The Chelsea Flower Show

The Chelsea

Faith and Geoff Whiten

with photographs by Derek Goard

Flower Show

Published in association with the Royal Horticultural Society

ELM TREE BOOKS . London

For Dominic and Josh again

First published in Great Britain 1982
by Elm Tree Books/Hamish Hamilton Ltd
Garden House 57-59 Long Acre London WC2E 9JZ

Copyright © 1982 by Faith and Geoff Whiten

Book design by Norman Reynolds

British Library Cataloguing in Publication Data
Whiten, Faith,
 The Chelsea Flower Show.
 1. Chelsea Flower Show—History
 I. Title   II. Whiten, Geoff
 35'.07402134   SB403.Z5
 ISBN 0-241-10744-X

Filmset by Pioneer
Printed and bound in Great Britain by
Billing & Sons Ltd,
Guildford, London, Oxford, Worcester

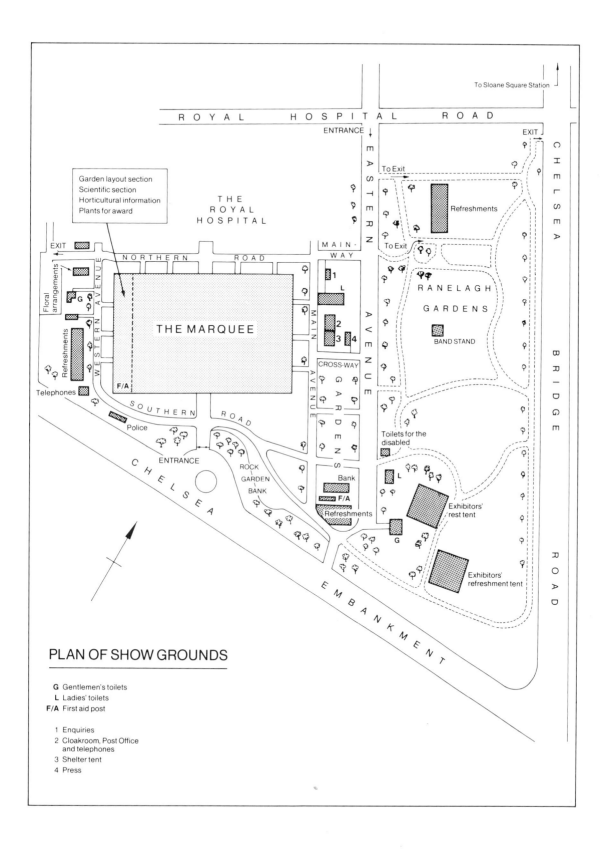

ROYAL HOSPITAL ROAD

To Sloane Square Station

ENTRANCE

EXIT

Garden layout section
Scientific section
Horticultural information
Plants for award

THE ROYAL HOSPITAL

To Exit

Refreshments

EXIT

NORTHERN ROAD

MAIN-WAY

To Exit

Floral arrangements

1

EASTERN AVENUE

G

WESTERN AVENUE

L

RANELAGH GARDENS

BAND STAND

Refreshments

THE MARQUEE

2
3   4

MAIN AVENUE

CHELSEA BRIDGE ROAD

Telephones

F/A

CROSS-WAY

GARDENS

SOUTHERN ROAD

Toilets for the disabled

Police

ENTRANCE

ROCK GARDEN BANK

L

Bank

F/A

Refreshments

Exhibitors' rest tent

G

CHELSEA EMBANKMENT

Exhibitors' refreshment tent

PLAN OF SHOW GROUNDS

G Gentlemen's toilets
L Ladies' toilets
F/A First aid post

1 Enquiries
2 Cloakroom, Post Office and telephones
3 Shelter tent
4 Press

ACKNOWLEDGEMENTS

The authors and publishers would like to thank the following for their help in the preparation of this book.

All the photographs, with the exception of those acknowledged below, were taken by Derek Goard, to whom very many thanks.

Central Press Photos for photographs on pages 27, 28, 40 and 83.

Sport & General Press Agency for photographs on pages 30, 32 and 38

Fox Photos Ltd for the photograph on page 93.

Mike Warren for the colour photograph of the Central Royal Parks exhibit.

Dominic Whiten for the photograph on page 63.

And for their assistance in researching the text: The Lord Aberconway, John Cowell, John Mattock and members of the Shows Committee, Allan Sawyer and the staff of the Shows Office, Mr Stageman and Dr Elliott of the Lindley Library, Mr Michael Raymer of the Royal Hospital, Mr and Mrs Sargent, Mr Fred Potter, Michael Lumley, Peter Seabrook, Julia Clements and David Mann.

Two publications: *The Story of the Royal Horticultural Society* by H.R. Fletcher, based on research by A. Simmonds, and the *Gardener's Chronicle* magazine, were also particularly helpful.

Illustrations for the chapter openings are taken from the *Handbook of Plant and Floral Ornament* by Richard G. Hatton.

Every effort has been made to acknowledge all those who have assisted in the preparation of this book. Should there be any omissions in this respect, we apologise and shall be pleased to make the appropriate acknowledgement in future editions.

FOREWORD

To those who have been to the Chelsea Flower Show, and to those who have not, this book will appeal equally, but for different reasons. The latter will find their appetites irresistibly whetted: the former will not only enjoy the evocative mood of Chelsea conveyed by the tone of the book, but will be fascinated by the scenario, graphically but lightly described, of the build-up to the show, and what is involved for the organisers and the exhibitors.

The excitements, the hopes, the misgivings, the toil and the fun of exhibiting is known at first hand by the writers who for several years past have constructed at Chelsea novel, well thought out small gardens, for one of which, though modestly they refrain from saying so, they triumphantly won a Gold Medal.

Their skill in devising and constructing a garden is matched by their skill in researching their material for this book, in arranging it, and in presenting it in a style amusing and compelling, yet natural.

Although the Royal Horticultural Society is happy to be associated with this book, the Society did not commission it. It is the Whitens' book, showing, as they see it, the more fascinating facets of the world's most famous flower show. Even so, their personal reactions are kept in proportion, so that the whole, showing the evolution of Chelsea from 1912, is a rounded, accurate work.

I warmly congratulate the authors, and equally warmly commend the book. Vividly evocative of past shows, and mouthwateringly anticipatory of the next, it will make excellent winter reading: for if winter comes, can the Great Spring Show be far behind?

The Lord Aberconway, 1982

CHAPTER 1

OR MOST of the year, the grounds of the Royal Hospital in Chelsea, home of the famous Chelsea Pensioners, has the peaceful, green appearance of any of the public open spaces for which London is renowned. Beyond the heavy metal railings, traffic constantly roars along the Chelsea Embankment and across the Thames rise the tall trees of Battersea Park and taller chimneys of Battersea Power Station.

In these grounds local residents walk their well-coiffed dogs, jog or quietly sunbathe; mothers and nannies accompany scampering or roller-skating off-spring or push sedate prams; a game of football may be in progress; a pair of elderly gentlemen in beribboned blue serge coats stroll and reminisce.

But for forty days each year, a dramatic transformation occurs, starting at a steady pace, then gradually quickening to a frenzied, bustling crescendo of brilliant colour that is sustained for a brief four days before apparently disappearing whence it came, leaving hardly a trace.

The significance of forty days as a Biblical timespan could almost be by design, for what occurs is surely some sort of miracle. If one is nearer God's heart in a garden than anywhere else on earth, then the journey to this small park can be considered a pilgrimage of the faithful, for here, each May, is the home of the world's most famous and prestigious flower show — the Chelsea Show.

A London cab driver once said, 'When the Chelsea Show comes round, we reckon that summer's really arrived.' The weather may not always agree, but Chelsea is indeed an event essential to the British summer, like Ascot, Wimbledon or the Derby, and is associated with two subjects dear to the British heart — gardening and Royalty. This is an occasion when the best of gardening from this country and abroad is seen by many members of the Royal family, as well as some 250,000 gardeners, ranging from the fanatical to the idly curious.

Flower shows are traditionally held by any town or village horticultural society worth its salt; what makes Chelsea so special is not just its size, but its authority and diversity. The Great Marquee contains three-and-a-half acres of plants and flowers of almost every description ranged in stunning, perfumed splendour, as well as a garden layout section with plans and photographs and scientific displays where gardening problems are solved. Outside are full scale gardens with lawns, patios, pools or mountain streams; a flamboyance of floral art; equipment ranging from greenhouses, ladders and ride-on mowers to sprayers, trowels and cloches; sundries such as books, flower pots, herbicides, pesticides and fertilisers and, for the leisurely gardener, loungers, hammocks, seats and barbecues.

But, for all its diversity, Chelsea remains loyal to its horticultural purpose, for this is the show not of any common or garden club, but the Royal Horticultural Society, an august institution of the old school that is regarded with both affection and respect. As upholder of the pursuit of excellence, fountain of awards and rewards, and guardian of the best traditions, the RHS evinces a sense of security and continuity in a changing world.

Gardeners are, by and large, friendly, benevolent souls and although inevitable disagreements arise from time to time between the Society's Council and its 70,000-odd members, there exists a sense of companionship and enthusiasm that pervades the atmosphere even of its largest show.

The RHS has held its Great Spring Show at Chelsea since 1913, with short breaks only during some of the years of both World Wars. In terms of the Society's history, this is but a comparatively short span. It now has a considerable establishment, with offices, halls and a library in Westminster, a garden at Wisley famous for its research and training facilities, and a thriving publishing and trading arm. But this has not always been the case, for the Society has endured somewhat chequered fortunes since it was founded by the germ of an idea in the mind of just one man in 1801 — an idea that came to fruition at a meeting of a select half-a-dozen men at the premises of a Mr Hatchard, bookseller, of 187 Piccadilly, on 7 March 1804. The meeting is commemorated by a plaque on the wall of Hatchards Bookshop, still on the same site.

In 1804, railways did not exist, and the general method of transport was stage-coach or horseback. King George III was on the throne and Britain was at war with Napoleon's France. In nearly every English county there were already societies for the improvement of agriculture, but none specifically for the improvement of horticulture. The suggestion for the formation of a horticultural society came not from a leading botanist, but from the son of a potter who had entered banking. John Wedgwood was the eldest son of Josiah Wedgwood,

John Wedgwood, one of the founders of the Royal Horticultural Society

founder of the famous pottery, who had decided that the family business was not for him. In 1804 he lived at Cote House, Durdham Down near Bristol, where he enthusiastically grew exotic fruit and plants under glass, as well as many flowers, and had planted an orchard. He had called for advice on his garden from William Forsyth, gardener to King George III at two Royal establishments, Kensington and St James's. Forsyth was considered an authority on fruit trees, having produced a book on their cultivation and management, but his most remarkable claim to fame seems to be that he succeeded in obtaining a Government grant for no less than £1,500 for the secret of making and applying a 'Plaister', of which the main ingredients were cow dung, lime-rubbish (preferably from old ceilings) and wood-ash. This concoction was supposed to have remarkable powers for healing wounds in trees.

On 29 June 1801, Wedgwood wrote to Forsyth, explaining that he had been considering the formation of a horticultural society, the main object of which would be 'to collect every information respecting the culture and treatment of all plants and trees, as well culinary as ornamental.' During the next month the letter was passed on by Forsyth to Sir Joseph Banks, a revered scientific authority, Life President of the Royal Society and a personal friend and advisor to the King. As a young man, Banks had persuaded the Admiralty to allow him, with a staff of seven and at his own expense, to join Cook's first major voyage in 1768, as a naturalist. The specimens and information he had brought back had established his reputation.

Banks welcomed Wedgwood's suggestion with enthusiasm, returning the letter to Forsyth with the comment, 'I approve very much the idea. I know of no trade that conceals so many valuable branches of knowledge as that of a gardener, and few subjects where the public will be more benefited by the disclosures which such a society will occasion.' This comment has proved to be one of remarkable perspicacity. Although the trade of 'gardener' has altered considerably, the disclosure of gardening information to the public has become the essence of the Chelsea Show.

Banks has been described as 'the greatest botanical and horticultural impresario the world has ever known.' He would probably approve of a show as spectacular and as world-renowned as Chelsea is today. Although he was already in his sixties when the Society was formed, he gave it loyal and generous support — often at his own expense — for the rest of his life, and was also highly influential in establishing Kew Gardens and the Chelsea Physic Garden.

The name of Banks is well remembered, for shortly after his death in 1820 the Banksian Medal was struck in his honour, to be awarded to exhibits of sufficient merit shown at the meetings of the Society, and the Silver and Silver Gilt medals are still awarded to exhibitors of gardens and plants at Chelsea.

The Banksian Medals may provide a sense of continuity between the Society's early meetings and its 20th century shows, but exhibits of flowers and plants played a much less important role at that time. Chelsea is now the zenith of the RHS shows — its biggest and brightest — but smaller, indoor shows are held regularly throughout most of the year at the Halls in Westminster, where, but a short walk from the bustle of Victoria Station and the offices of Whitehall, it is possible to enjoy for a while the gentle colour, perfume and atmosphere more closely associated with an English country garden.

Sir Joseph Banks

In the formative years of the early 1800s, many papers were read to the Society's meetings by members, but surprisingly, any kind of exhibit was most unusual. The first to be recorded was not some new, exotic flower, but a humble potato, shown in April 1805 by Mr Minier. The notable characteristic of the 'Potatoe' in question was that 'its tubers form so late in the season and have so thin a skin that they may be used through the winter, like young Potatoes.'

Much of the Society's early business concentrated on fruit and vegetables. There was considerable interest at the time in the cultivation of exotic fruit under glass, and great competition between members to produce the biggest and best fruit for dessert at the Society's annual Anniversary Dinner. In 1822, for instance, when the dinner was held at the Freemasons' Tavern in Lincoln's Inn Fields, the Marquis of Hertford's gardener, Mr Thomas Baldwin, sent four huge pineapples, one of which weighed 8lb 14oz.

Membership of the Society (or Fellowship as it was by then called) was restricted to men until 1830, but the fame of the displays of fruit at the Anniversary Dinner had spread, and non-Fellows, including ladies, were anxious to see the spectacle. Eventually the Council succumbed to their arguments, and a limited number of spectators were allowed into the gallery during the meal.

In spite of the competitive spirit among those who grew fruit, the Society was anxious to avoid jealousy and bad feeling between Fellows who exhibited at the meetings, and so, in sharp contrast to today, when it has the discretion to bestow many and varied awards upon Members, show exhibitors and plants, it avowed to remain completely impartial, declaring that the thanks given to those who presented exhibits or read Papers at its meetings 'are to be considered in no other light than as a matter of civility.' This rather stuffy attitude was, however, relatively short-lived, for by 1858 awards to specific plants were instigated, as guidance to gardeners considering the worth of new introductions.

If the Royal Horticultural Society is today the revered and august body that its name suggests, things appear to have been rather different in 1825. It is

Caricature by George Cruikshank of a meeting of the Society in the 'Great Room' in 1825

EXHIBITION EXTRAORDINARY in the HORTICULTURAL ROOM.

Dr John Lindley

hardly conceivable now that any journal would have the temerity to produce a cartoon as wickedly, irreverently amusing as the caricature by George Cruikshank, well known cartoonist of the time — nor, perhaps, in fairness would any wish to do so. The coloured etching is entitled 'Exhibition Extraordinary in the Horticultural Room' and depicts a meeting in the 'Great Room', situated to the rear of the Society's premises at 21 Lower Regent Street, close to Jermyn Street — later partially occupied by the Plaza Cinema.

Many of the figures caricatured were not directly connected with the Horticultural Society, but would have been familiar through their association with various scandals and political intrigues of the time. However, one figure whose connection was both direct and disastrous is John Turner (wearing spectacles and seated to the left of the Chairman). Turner was Assistant Secretary, and having a fairly free hand with the accounts, he systematically embezzled funds that eventually totalled some £1,000. Upon final discovery of his crimes he fled to France. The caption under his name in Cruikshank's cartoon reads, 'An highly cultivated specimen — requires glass.' But in a later edition the pertinent footnote 'Now transplanted to a warmer Climate' was added.

One of the reasons for lack of control over Turner's activities was that the Honorary Secretary, Joseph Sabine, was devoting almost all his attentions to the development of the Society's Garden, on a site of thirty-three acres at Chiswick, leased from the Duke of Devonshire, who resided at Chiswick House. The lease was taken out in 1821, and within a few years, a wide variety of plants was established. The range of fruit and vegetables (3,825 varieties of fruit alone) was colossal, but ornamental plants were not neglected. As well as paeonies, phloxes, irises and a collection of 1200 roses, there were plants newly introduced to the country such as chrysanthemum, orchids and the very first camellia — all from China. Greenhouse and stove plants had been brought back by intrepid pioneer collectors from India, South America and the West Indies, many of these expeditions having been sponsored by the Society.

The Chiswick garden was not only a show piece; it led the country both in its horticultural research and experiments, and in its innovation of training young men as gardeners. But, successful as the garden was, it was also expensive to run. Moreover, the misdeeds of Turner had shaken public confidence in the Society, and to add to its financial problems, many Fellows were remiss in their payment of subscriptions, being anything up to three years overdue.

In 1827, as an economy measure, the Anniversary Dinner was replaced by a Horticultural Fete at Chiswick, with refreshments and a military band. This proved highly successful, and for a while became an annual Society event, although in 1829 disaster struck in the form of a fierce thunderstorm. Even now, rain can turn Chelsea into a very muddy experience, but at Chiswick the scene was pandemonium. Hundreds of people thronged to shelter in the small marquees, and were stuck in the entrances. Those inside hardly fared better, as the tents were in a valley. According to the *Morning Post*, visitors were 'nearly ankle deep in water oozing from the gravel; shrieks were dreadful, and the loss of shoes particularly annoying.' However, the British spirit refused, then as

The Horticultural Fate dedicated to the Rainer Family

"The kindly dew drops form the higher tree . "Our gayness and our gear are all besmirch'd ...
And wels the little plants that nestle underneath

'The Horticultural Fate'
at Chiswick in 1829

now, to be dampened by the elements, and men could be seen triumphantly bearing from the caterer's establishment dishes of meats and fruits, held in their umbrellas — as well as bottles of champagne, claret, Burgundy and Madeira!

Soon after this, under the guidance of John Lindley, Assistant Secretary both to the Society and its garden, the Horticultural Society's shows began to take on a better organised and more seriously horticultural nature. Until 1831, exhibits at the meetings in London had been haphazard affairs, with Fellows bringing any item that they thought might be interesting. Then, at Lindley's suggestion, a series of proper competitions was held — with medals awarded to pineapples in February; camellias in April; rhododendrons in May; azaleas, roses and grapes in June; pineapples and melons in July, and dahlias, roses and grapes in September. Lindley was a brilliant, imaginative man with an apparently boundless capacity for hard work, in spite of having lost the use of one eye in childhood. He was the son of a Norfolk nurseryman, and had started his career with the Society at the Chiswick garden. He eventually became Secretary, as well as being Professor of Botany at University College, London and helping to edit the *Gardener's Chronicle* magazine. On his death, his library was purchased by the RHS, and formed the nucleus of its Lindley Library, now housed at Vincent Square. A Lindley Medal was also struck, (after some difficulty in achieving a sufficiently good likeness) and is still awarded to 'an exhibit of a plant or plants of special interest or beauty, or showing exceptional skill in cultivation, and for educational exhibits.'

The competitions instigated by Lindley eventually proved so popular that they outgrew their indoor venue, and so it was decided to hold three shows — in May, June and July respectively — under canvas at the Chiswick garden, with a

The Society's Garden at Kensington in 1862

fourth in September eventually being added. Little wonder that these events attracted great crowds, for with the delights of the garden itself alongside exhibits of some of the country's finest fruits and flowers, the provision of refreshments and the accompaniment of bands of music, the atmosphere must have been very similar to that of early Chelsea Shows. There was apparently a social as well as horticultural appeal, for as the *Gardener's Magazine* pointed out, 'the principal part of the English aristocracy are present, and mix indiscriminately with the tradesman, the mechanic and the gardener. This scene may be enjoyed by men, women and children, for five or six hours, at 3s 6d each.'

In spite of the continued success and increasing prestige of the Chiswick shows for some twenty-five years, during the same period the Society was simply not able to balance its books. Its financial situation had not really recovered from the borrowing necessitated by the Turner episode, and things went from bad to worse — so much worse that by 1858 not only had the Chiswick shows ceased but the splendid Regent Street office had to be sold.

Also in this year, both the Secretary and the President, the Duke of Devonshire, died, and the latter was succeeded as President by an even more illustrious figure — His Royal Highness, the Prince Consort.

It was decided to leave the Chiswick garden purely as an experimental establishment, and to seek a site nearer to the centre of London for a show garden and exhibition venue. Under Prince Albert's guidance, the chosen site

16

that was duly developed was a plot of twenty acres of land at Kensington Gore situated between Kensington, Cromwell, Exhibition and Prince Albert Roads, and leased from the Royal Commissioners. The Natural History Museum now stands on part of this site.

Unfortunately, in this development — undertaken with financial help from the Royal Commissioners as well as donations from Queen Victoria, Prince Albert and others — the Society allowed itself to be diverted from strictly horticultural concerns, and became carried away with the Prince Consort's fondness for Italian arcades and canals, formal statuary and expensive works of art. However, his influence and enthusiasm for the Society did result in the enrolment of many new Fellows, and finances began to improve.

The Prince formally opened the still unfinished gardens in June 1861, an event attended by another eight members of the Royal family and such distinguished personages as Lord Palmerston, Disraeli and Gladstone. But seven months later the Prince was dead, and in spite of Queen Victoria's sympathetic interest, once again the Society's fortunes began to founder.

It was eventually realised that the Royal Horticultural Society, as it had become under the Queen's patronage, had rather lost its way with the costly Kensington venture, although horticulture had by no means been entirely neglected. Many splendid flower shows were held there, not least the Great International Exhibition of 1862 and the International Horticultural Exhibition and Botanical Congress of 1866 — later to prove of some significance in the progress towards the first Chelsea Shows. But such facilities as a skating rink and tennis courts were felt to be the wrong attractions for a horticultural society's garden, and various disagreements between the RHS and the Royal Commissioners over the running of the garden eventually came to a head, resulting in the premises reverting to the control of the Commissioners and the Society relinquishing even its offices.

The removal was to a sorry two rooms in Victoria Street, and a location for shows was found in the unprepossessing venue of the London Scottish Drill Hall at Buckingham Gate. Surprisingly quickly, arrangements were also made for an outdoor show under canvas to be held in May 1888 at the Embankment Gardens of the Benchers of the Inner Temple, close to Charing Cross. This was only a two-day show, and the weather was appalling, but in spite of everything, the exhibitors had rallied round to produce a magnificent display, and attendance was good. The *Gardener's Chronicle* reported: 'On entering the long tent with its fine display of herbaceous plants and "market stuff", the visitor could scarcely refrain from an exclamation of delight and surprise.' A sentiment familiar to many people who remember their first glimpse inside the marquee at Chelsea!

As well as flowers, including lilies, lily of the valley, tulips, paeonies and orchids in abundance, there was fruit such as apples, mangoes, oranges, and grapes — much of it from Australia.

The Temple Show became an annual event, patronised by Royalty, and the fortunes of the Society slowly and steadily improved. It was these shows, with their several marquees containing exhibits of horticultural splendour, varied

facilities for refreshments and accompaniment of military band music, that set the pattern for Chelsea, and became its direct forerunner.

By the early 1900s relations between the RHS and the Templers had become rather strained. Many of the latter resented the noise, mud and, apparently, strong smells of cooking that emanated from the shows. The Society itself was successful and prosperous, celebrating a triumphant centenary in 1904 with the acquisition of sites for a Hall and offices in Vincent Square and for its own garden at Wisley, near Ripley, Surrey. Both ventures flourished under the care of the Secretary, Rev W. Wilks.

The final departure from the Temple to Chelsea was prompted not by one of the Society's own shows, but by the organisers of an event planned for May 1912 to rival the memorable Kensington show of 1866, and to be known as the Royal International Horticultural Exhibition.

The idea did originate from the Royal Horticultural Society itself, and was put forward by its President, Sir Trevor Lawrence, to a public meeting, following Press advertisements appealing to persons interested in horticulture. A Committee was appointed to organise the exhibition but, mindful of its great financial responsibilities, it soon formed itself into a limited liability company, inviting subscriptions to raise funds and guarantees to underwrite financial contingencies. Although the RHS did not participate directly in the organisation as a society, it did donate £1,000 towards expenses and guarantee £4,000 in the event of a loss being made. Moreover, its treasurer, Mr J. Gurney Fowler, was appointed Chairman, its secretary, the Rev W. Wilks served on the Board of Directors, and its resources and staff were put at the disposal of the organisers.

In return for this financial support, the RHS received for its Fellows a considerable reduction in entrance fees (these ranged from £2 2s on the first day to 1s on the last three), thus achieving what was described as 'another of those strokes of business which do so much to popularise the Society.'

Influential interest was soon aroused in the project, and the Duke of Portland became its President. Once again, members of the Royal Family gave their generous support to a horticultural exhibition, and patrons included King George, Queen Mary and Queen Alexandra.

Managing director was Mr Edward White, a member of the firm of Milner, Son & White, landscape gardeners, and a major task for him and his fellow directors was to find a suitable site. This must be near to the centre of London, accessible by public transport, and must offer sufficient area and facilities for an exhibition of considerable size, there being 1407 applications for space in the first instance. Eventually part of the grounds of the Royal Hospital, Chelsea was secured at a rent originally set at £500, and the great number of entries caused the actual space taken up to be expanded twice, eventually covering about twenty-eight acres.

Edward White was full of enthusiasm for the site: 'The position is ideal in many respects, among its advantages being two ample entrances from Queen's Road and the Chelsea Embankment respectively within a few minutes' walk from Sloane Square station.

'There is open space for tents covering nearly six acres, and there are in

OPPOSITE

Horticultural Fete visitors caricatured by Dower Wilson in 1879

addition several broad shaded avenues and the sheltered and mature gardens, which offer a good example of Middle Victorian landscape gardening and will make a perfect background for outdoor exhibits and the rock and water gardens.'

Surprisingly little of the intricate organisation involved in preparing and staging modern Chelsea Shows is officially documented. However, in 1912 one Reginald Cory, a wealthy and enthusiastic amateur gardener, had the foresight to record the Royal International Horticultural Exhibition for the benefit of posterity. The record is contained in a large, imposing bound volume with remarkable plates of flowers and gardens in muted pastel shades. One of the few remaining copies is in the possession of the Lindley Library.

Its ponderous title is *The Horticultural Record consisting of coloured and half-tone reproductions of the most interesting and valuable Flowers, Plants, Shrubs, Groups and Rock Gardens exhibited at the Royal International Horticultural Exhibition, 1912.* The volume is dedicated 'by special permission' to King George V and in its introduction, the editor hopes that the work will provide 'sufficient excuse for adding one more to the already countless books on gardening subjects.' Anyone who takes even passing note of the apparently constant stream of gardening publications that appear today will surely appreciate the poignancy of that particular comment!

One might expect the organisation of an exhibition that took place some seventy years ago to reveal marked, intriguing and even amusing differences from the way in which such an event would be staged today. But whilst refrigerated juggernauts may have replaced horse-drawn pantechnecons for the transportation of plants, and a range of sophisticated fertilisers and insecticides taken over in common use from the Ichthemic guano and cyanide fumes favoured by professional gardeners of the time, the detailed arrangements of staging a spectacular flower show at Chelsea have remained amazingly similar.

A glance through the Record reveals many of the familiar features — the post office and telephones, the St John Ambulance post, refreshment facilities, the vast marquee of some four acres and sundry smaller pavilions, these all being supplied by Piggot Bros who apparently 'gave the utmost satisfaction.' Plumbing and electricity, then as now, had to be laid on. Electric lighting to illuminate the entire grounds was installed at a cost of £600, and surface drains were laid to serve an area of ten acres. In the event, the weather was superb, but even the problems that this could have caused were foreseen, and water-carts were in constant use during the show. Then, as now, the assistance of the police was enlisted and, as a mark of appreciation for the 'efficient control of the public', the Directors presented £10 to the Police Orphan Fund.

Also then as now, the element of simple human error intruded to frustrate the best laid plans. One can but imagine the exasperated scenes involving visitors, impatient to see the delights of the show, but thwarted by what the *Gardener's Chronicle* called 'The "gate" difficulty of the opening day.'

There follows a letter from the Chairman of the Show's Directors, explaining the delay in opening the gates at the east entrance. 'The fullest investigation has been made,' he writes, 'and the omission to open the gate appears to have been due to a misunderstanding of instructions by one of the subordinate officials,

who, unfortunately interpreted the order given not to open the main entrance until after the departure of the Royal Party as applying to his gate also.

'To save any inconvenience, care was taken that the public should be directed to entrances other than the main one until it was open.'

The start of the show was marked by the visit of the Royal Party — notably King George and Queen Mary, although there was no formal opening function due to recent deaths in the Royal Family. This being an international exhibition, the preview was also attended by ambassadors from numerous countries. Particular emphasis is placed in the Record on the visit of one foreign party — that of their Royal Highnesses the Archduke and Archduchess Franz Ferdinand of Austria. (In view of the repercussions of the Duke's later assassination at Sarajevo and the dramatic effect of four years' war on almost every European country, this special mention reveals an almost uncanny prescience.)

The show that was seen by the sundry dignitaries and some thousands of members of the public over eight days was, by all accounts, magnificent. It had been a difficult year for growers, but in the marquee they still managed to produce the vast, breathtaking banks of apparently perfect flowers and foliage for which Chelsea has become renowned. The large groups of plants were staged not on tables or benches, but at ground level, so that the finished

The International Horticultural Exhibition in 1912. Original photographs from The Horticultural Record

21

impression was of beds in some impossibly extravagant garden, where the normal effects of time and the elements had been suspended, and where no harmful pest or disease would dare intrude to spoil the silent, scented splendour.

Most splendid of all, by general agreement, were the orchids — not only by virtue of their mysterious, exotic appearance but also by virtue of the skill employed by growers — notably Sir George Holford of Westonbirt and his gardeners — in artificially breeding new kinds of the flowers; an achievement considered impossible by a previous generation. The orchids even enjoyed the advantage of their own, specially heated marquee. Although Sir George's exhibit was almost priceless, less wealthy afficionados were not forgotten, for it was possible to order 100 orchids for £5, and produce one's own display of these fashionable flowers.

Progress had been made, too, in the breeding of roses, with Ramblers as the most recent introduction. The *Gardener's Chronicle* was in no doubt about its preference for the newcomers, reporting that 'A specimen rose used to be a large, stiffly-trained bush, with the flowers carefully tied an equal distance apart, suggesting almonds in a pudding. How very different are the graceful, airy examples that may be seen in the great tent at Chelsea today.'

Other popular attractions were the displays of rhododendrons, which by this time had become so well assimilated into the native garden that they were thought of as typically British plants. Late May sees many varieties of this stately, showy shrub in the peak of bloom, and superb rhododendrons have become essential to Chelsea — a feature no doubt influenced in recent years by the considerable knowledge and enthusiasm for the subject of Lord Aberconway, President of the Royal Horticultural Society, and of his father before him.

The Exhibition in 1912 boasted not only plant displays, but full-scale gardens — and in particular rock gardens. Many were rather fussy and ornate, or dotted with numerous small, colourful alpine plants, and some manifested the current enthusiasm for Japanese gardens, although it must be said that most seem to have demonstrated a uniquely English interpretation of the Japanese style,

Further photographs of the Avenue and the Marquee from The Horticultural Record

rather than anything much akin to the quiet, understated mood of the authentic setting.

Ornate garden decorations suited the mood of the period, and topiary was a popular feature of the show. One man who may be considered the doyen of the art bore the unbelievable name of Mr Cutbush, prompting the fruits of his creativity to be referred to as 'Mr Cutbush's cut bushes'.

The awards given to exhibitors of flowers, fruit, plants and gardens seem to have been almost as numerous as the exhibitors themselves, and the stand displaying the many trophies and cups almost as great an attraction. In addition, gold, silver and bronze medals were awarded, as well as diplomas and money prizes. Most coveted was the special cup given by His Majesty the King for the best exhibit in the show, which was awarded to Sir George Holford for his group of orchids.

But garden sundries and equipment were not neglected, and nowhere were the current fads and fashions of gardening more convincingly demonstrated than in these exhibits. Messrs H. Pattisson & Co of Streatham showed, for example, their 'well known horse boots for use on lawns etc', these being leather shoes to cover the hooves of horses drawing lawnmowers or rollers, and protect the grass.

Many of the exhibitors of equipment and machinery had London premises, and many of their products were concerned with greenhouses. The Twelve Hours Stove Syndicate of Vauxhall Bridge Road, for example, showed their patent greenhouse boilers, of powers ranging from forty to 700 feet of piping. Greater sophistication was introduced by Chas. P. Kinnell & Co of Southwark Street, whose Anglian Boiler was fitted with rocking bars 'for the better cleaning of the fire-bed.' From further afield, came a means of fuelling the boilers, as the Pwllbach Colliery Co Ltd of Swansea showed an enormous block of its anthracite coal. From a very much greater distance came an exhibit of ventilating gear by the Quaker City Machine Co of Richmond, Indiana, USA. Their system was controlled by a pair of cog-wheels with bicycle chain.

Means of controlling plant pests and diseases were even less sophisticated. Price's Candle Co of Battersea offered a preparation of soft soap and quassia which, mixed with boiling water and allowed to stand for 24 hours, acted as a cleanser and insecticide. For fumigating the greenhouse, there was Mr Edwards' of Leeds patent cyaniding machine. Reassuringly, this was arranged by clockwork, so that a scoop trap containing cyanide was emptied into a tank of water and sulphuric acid fifty seconds after the clockwork was started, 'thus enabling the operator to escape the fumes.'

Neither was the ornamental aspect of gardens forgotten, with Liberty's of Regent Street exhibiting one of the most appealing and romantic displays. In what was described as a very long summerhouse were numerous Japanese garden ornaments — old bronze lanterns six feet high, granite arches and gate-posts with Japanese inscriptions, delicately chiselled bronze storks and bamboo gates and bungalows. There were even plants that predicted the regular exhibits of bonsai trees at modern shows — 'healthy dwarfed Cupressus obtusa growing in very old-looking vases.' The *Gardener's Chronicle* report continues that 'from the roof quaint lanterns were suspended, and after dusk the various lanterns in this interesting arrangement gave it a very Oriental effect.'

Such a wealth of tantalising beauty and intriguing ideas could hardly fail to entice — and, having enticed, to captivate. The Exhibition was attended by just over 178,000 people, the weather was perfect, there was a profit of £2,668 2s 5d to be donated to charities, and the show was declared a signal success. Managing director Edward White reported that 'Although it is quite conceivable that the success of 1912 may be surpassed at some future date, it is indisputable that the Exhibition held that year was a distinct advance upon all previous efforts of the kind.'

What other sensible course of action was there for the RHS than to announce the grounds of the Royal Hospital, Chelsea as the venue for its own Spring Show in 1913? The site works had been undertaken, the necessary facilities had been tried and tested, and the exhibition had proved that a show at Chelsea would attract exhibitors and visitors alike and — perhaps most importantly — prove a financial success.

CHAPTER 2

T O THE Royal Horticultural Society, the new venue for its Great Spring Show proved a form of salvation. Grateful though the Society was to the Benchers of the Inner Temple for the use of the Temple Gardens, the highly successful shows there had outgrown the site, becoming cramped and uncomfortable. The South Grounds of the Royal Hospital, Chelsea offered three times the amount of space and the number of exhibitors who made application for the 1913 show was nearly double that of the last Temple show in 1911. Moreover, luncheon was to be served (a facility impossible at the Temple) and in case 'City men' were in doubt about access to the new location, it was pointed out that they could take the District Railway from Mansion House to Sloane Square station.

Success was anticipated, but on 24 May 1913 the *Gardener's Chronicle* reported: 'The success of the exhibition of the Royal Horticultural Society, which opened on Tuesday last in the grounds of the Royal Hospital Chelsea, has exceeded all expectations. The brilliant appearance in the two-acre tent brought vividly back to mind the glories of the great show of last season, and it seemed that we were again witnessing an international display of the world's horticulture, so large and numerous were the groups, and so magnificent the quality of the varied exhibits.'

Among the exhibitors at that first Chelsea Show were names that are still familiar to gardeners and Chelsea Show visitors. Blackmore and Langdon of

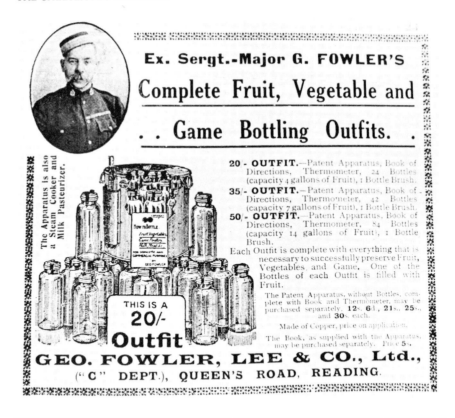

*Advertisements from
the 1914 Chelsea Show
Catalogue*

Bath were already famed for their double-flowered, tuberous begonias, which they brought to the Show wrapped in cotton wool. Mr Blackmore and Mr Langdon had entered into partnership in 1901 and three years later started to breed those fantastic delphiniums for which they are still renowned.

Rhododendrons were shown by Messrs John Waterer & Sons of Bagshot and by Mr G. Reuthe of Keston, among others. Members of the Waterer family had carried out pioneering work in the hybridisation of rhododendrons (particularly the group known as the Knaphill azaleas after the Waterer nursery in Woking) since the mid 1800s. In 1913 John Waterer was continuing the family tradition with these plants at his Bagshot nursery, and exporting in great quantity to the United States, but within the next year his nursery amalgamated with the Wargrave Hardy Plant Farm and so took the name of John Waterer Sons & Crisp Ltd — a name renowned for its nursery, garden centre and landscaping activities, and still trading from the same nursery in Bagshot. Reuthe was a much smaller business that has remained a family concern, with nurseries both at Keston and Ightham in Kent still producing and showing rhododendrons and azaleas.

A wider selection of shrubs was shown by Mr R.C. Notcutt, whose descendant Mr Charles Notcutt is now managing director of the substantial company of Notcutts Nurseries Ltd, with extensive tree and shrub nurseries in and around Woodbridge, Suffolk, six garden centres in East Anglia and Birmingham and an active landscaping branch.

Closer examination of Blackmore and Langdon's famous begonias

Another Kent firm, then based at nearby Chislehurst but now in Knockholt, was Whiteleggs — then known as Whitelegg and Page — who showed in 1913 a bold rock garden made from Tonbridge stone, which the *Gardener's Chronicle* found 'rather raw and crude and yellow'. In the years to follow Mr George Whitelegg showed many splendid rock gardens at Chelsea that met with much more general approbation, for he was regarded as a doyen of the art, and his son Richard still runs the company and regularly participates in Chelsea.

Mr Will Ingwersen of the alpine nursery in Gravetye, Sussex that bears his family name, holds the distinction of having been present in person at the first Chelsea Show as a child, helping to stage the family exhibit. Both he and his displays of tiny, exquisite alpine and rock plants in the marquee are still familiar to Chelsea visitors, and Mr Ingwersen has served on many of the Society's Committees as well as its Council. He is now a Vice-President.

The name of Allwood is inextricably linked with carnations. At Chelsea today the firm's stand is always close to the Main Avenue side of the marquee and is always a mass of colour and perfume with every shade imaginable of carnations and pinks. The nursery is now in Hassocks, but in 1913 the company was based at Haywards Heath and showed their 'delightfully scented' carnation 'Mary Allwood' and a variety that reflected the times by being named 'Empire Day'.

There was also a very different exhibitor at the 1913 show — a firm that still shows at Chelsea, although less well known than the big nurseries and plant exhibitors. E. H. Taylor Ltd supplies bee-keeping equipment from its base at Beehive Works, Welwyn, and was founded in 1880. From the company's Chelsea stand it is still possible to order bee hives, honey tanks, veils, gloves and

*Rock garden by
Mr George Whitelegg*

bee suits, wax extractors and even labels for your honey jars.

If the first Chelsea Show was voted a success, the second in 1914 was even more rapturously received, with improvements attributed to exhibitors and organisers having become accustomed to the site and to the exceptionally good weather of the season. That the Show should appear on such a high note was sadly ironic, because by 4 August Europe was at war.

On the very first day of the war the Society sprung into action, sending a letter to the Press pointing out the urgent necessity for increasing the nation's production of fruit and vegetables, and closely following it with the free issue of 100,000 leaflets explaining how this could be done in order to produce crops by the following winter. Then a total of twenty-one War Pamphlets were published, giving more specific advice and information on cropping gardens, and the Society went on to persuade the Government to grant powers to local authorities, under the Defence of the Realm Act, to put waste lands under cultivation.

For the next two years no effort seemed to be spared. Large quantities of plants and seeds of fruit and vegetables were purchased and sent to British Base Hospitals and Camps in France for planting there, and to prisoners of war in Germany; a sale of plants, books and sundries held at Vincent Square raised over £2,000 for the Red Cross Society, and a formidable committee of ladies raised £14,000 for the Society's War Relief Fund, including collections made at the Chelsea Show. In the midst of war, the Society combined with the Royal Agricultural Society to send an agent to Serbia, and on his advice despatched a large consignment of seeds. However, Serbia was overrun before the consignment reached its borders and so the seeds were distributed among British and French troops in Salonika and Malta.

In response to the horrendous number of casualties and the terrible injuries suffered by soldiers, the RHS accepted an invitation to help with laying out and planting cemeteries in France when the war was over, and offered to train disabled officers in horticulture in addition to planting the 'Star and Garter' hostel at Richmond for the incurably wounded.

As well as all this activity, the shows continued. The Chelsea Show was held in 1915 and 1916, although in the latter year economies were made by awarding only medals and not cups, and by making do with a series of large marquees instead of the Great Tent. However, with relentless optimism, it was asserted that the Council felt that this change 'might even serve to break a threatened monotony of repetition.' But by 1917 it was impossible to continue and Chelsea was cancelled 'on patriotic grounds'. In its place a small, indoor show was held at the London Scottish Drill Hall, Buckingham Gate, which was once again being used by the Society since its own Hall in Vincent Square was occupied by soldiers of the Australian Imperial Force. Mysteriously, the Australians by all accounts did not vacate the Hall until October, 1919 — nearly a year after the war was over — but at the beginning of that year the Society's Secretary, Rev W. Wilks, started to ask prospective exhibitors whether they could take space if a Chelsea Show were staged, and in a few brief months the Show was organised.

Of necessity, it was a subdued affair. The nation was hardly in a mood to celebrate the loss of 'the Flower of its Youth', although visitors did welcome the cheering effect of the blooms. The Society had determined to make the Show as educative as possible, and there were many scientific and educational exhibits as well as the usual shrubs, flowers and even rock gardens.

The *Gardener's Chronicle* reported that the many Belgian, French and Dutch horticulturists present 'expressed surprise at the extent and importance of the Show', but the magazine itself was surprised that, in spite of the importance of food production, there were only two exhibitors in the fruit and vegetable section. Of those two exhibitors, one was Messrs Suttons and Sons, the renowned Reading-based seed house, whose stand 'it need scarcely be said . . . . was as near perfection as is humanly possible.' Suttons had been present at the 1912 exhibition, and at every Chelsea Show so far, but the decade that was to follow saw the firm's exhibits in what might be considered to be their heyday.

One of the Social Events of the Season

The war had brought about social change as well as numbing grief, and the character of the 1920s was different from the 'long garden party' that preceded 1914. But although adaptations had to be made, the old social order of the estate owner served by the head gardener and a team of working gardeners remained intact for some years yet.

The first day of the Chelsea Show was attended by the gentry, members of the aristocracy and those who owned large country houses and estates with extensive gardens. Usually they would tour the Show with their head gardener, discussing new plants, placing orders for trees and shrubs to be delivered during the next autumn or winter, for a new greenhouse to be made to their own precise specifications or for quantities of seed for both vegetables and flowers. Carpet bedding and the herbaceous border were still extremely popular, and contributed a good deal to the work of the under gardeners responsible for maintenance.

The under gardeners themselves, together with their families and other working people from all walks of life, would attend the Show towards the end of the week, when admission was much cheaper. For those living some distance away, a 'charabanc' outing might be organised, but many gardeners working at the large country houses never saw the Show, either because they could not be spared at a busy time of year, or because there was no means of transport, for the gardeners would live in the 'bothy' or hostel on the estate from an early age, as they received their professional training.

It was in this climate that the nurserymen and seed houses showed their wares. As the head gardeners were experts in their own profession, so were the staff of the nurseries and seedsmen, and one who remembers those days vividly is Fred Potter. Mr Potter was with Suttons Seeds for sixty-three years until his retirement in 1980. For a good portion of that time he was responsible for breeding, trials and seed production of vegetables, and served on the Council of the RHS for ten years.

Mr Potter remembers that the company's Chelsea exhibits of the late 1920s were orchestrated by the late E.R. Janes, a master of showmanship who revolutionised staging techniques, introducing semi-circular bays, towers and cones of vegetables and covering the Monument in the marquee with vast mountains of flowers. He would sit on a box close to the stand and direct operations, with a staff of ten or twelve working day and night, but he looked after his staff well, who in turn respected him.

Growing and preparation for the Suttons exhibits started in August of the previous year. Flowers were forced under glass, with special tall houses for sweet peas, and seed was sown for more than twice the quantity of vegetables that would actually be needed, to ensure that there was sufficient produce in prime condition. On the Thursday before Chelsea week, root vegetables were lifted, washed, their roots trimmed where appropriate, and each root or tuber immediately wrapped in tissue paper to prevent discoloration. When it came to loading, resident carpenters would stand by and as the produce was carefully stacked into furniture pantechnecons — some twelve or thirteen in all — they would fix shelves and supports to prevent any damage. The pantechnecons were loaded from Thursday morning onwards and started their journey from Thursday night or Friday morning, with the last load being made on Sunday evening to leave early on Monday morning. The pantechnecons were drawn by two horses to Reading station where they were loaded on to the train, then carried across London from Paddington to Chelsea, again by horse. (This method of transport was common to most exhibitors and Railway inspectors even had an office at the Show.) All was timed and planned so that the material destined for the top of the exhibit arrived first, with that for the finishing touches bringing up the rear on Monday morning.

At the Show, the influence of the estate owners was great indeed. Fred Potter remembers, 'One head gardener was always in trouble because his nemesia lacked a proportion of blues. In order to satisfy this one owner, Suttons added more blue to their mixture and the flower seed director even visited the garden to make sure that the blues were in the correct proportion.'

There was terrific and fierce rivalry between the big seed houses at Chelsea — Suttons, Webbs, Carter and Toogood — particularly in the matter of the Sherwood Cup, which used to be awarded to the best exhibit in the Show. The four would always avoid staging a similar group, obviously engaging in prior discussion, but eventually competition for the cup became so controversial that it ceased to be awarded.

Evidence of the slowly changing scene came in 1926 when, due to the

General Strike, the tent contractors and garden exhibitors were 'greatly hindered' in getting their materials delivered, and in the end it became necessary to postpone the Show for a week. However, even this had a brighter side as the weather was abysmal on the original dates, but fine for the three days on which the Show was finally open. The Society had extended the previous year's Show to take in five days — a decision that proved unpopular with exhibitors, who were in the main prevented from showing cut flowers as they would not last.

The end of the 1920s saw the start of the career of a man whose long and loyal service to the Chelsea Show was to prove invaluable. In 1929 work was difficult to find and a young man called Ronald F. Sargent who had just left school was pleased to be sent — although along with thirty other applicants — for an interview with Col F.R. Durham, Secretary of the Royal Horticultural Society. Almost by luck, he was given the job of office boy. Although not on the Shows staff, Ron Sargent remembers attending Chelsea in 1929 where one of the most sensational exhibits was a collection of cacti and desert plants — still quite unfamiliar to British eyes — shown by Mr A. Sherman Hoyt from California.

Mr Sargent became an assistant in the Shows Office in 1934 and was involved in the organisation of every Chelsea Show from that time on. In 1951, he eventually became Shows Secretary, and in the late 1960s was joined by his wife, who was to be his temporary, part-time assistant — a job that lasted nine years! He retired in 1978, but is remembered by exhibitors with great affection, and by the RHS for his unerring loyalty and unfailingly modest and conscientious approach to his work. It seemed to him, he says, that exhibitors really pulled the stops out for his last Show — particularly the Royal Parks, who called their exhibit of a lock gate surrounded by dense planting, 'Sargent's Lock'. The lock keeper now enjoys an active retirement devoted in part to his great horticultural

A typical display of vegetables by Toogood — one of the great seed houses

passion — fruit and vegetables.

When Ron Sargent joined the staff of the Shows Office in 1934, it was under Mr A. Simmonds, who was Assistant Secretary responsible for Shows, and a formidable character — but one who was to make an important and lasting contribution to the Society. Mr Simmonds had been a student, and then a demonstrator, at Wisley before 1914 and had gained the highest marks in the first ever examination of the National Diploma of Horticulture. In the war he served in the machine gun corps and reached the rank of major, seeing fierce fighting and eventually being awarded the Military Cross.

Among his subordinates, it was felt that the terrible experiences of the war had taken their toll on Mr Simmonds' character, for he became what would now be known as a 'workaholic', spending long hours at his job and devoting to it a total dedication that he also unfortunately demanded from those less able or willing to do so. In short, he was something of a terror, but an efficient one who was always fair. His own secretary of the late 1940s remembers Mr Simmonds marching purposefully around the grounds at Chelsea, followed by a group of young ladies with notebooks, struggling to keep up with him and take down his rapidly dictated orders. Woe betide any exhibitor who stepped out of line. Experienced exhibitors always applied for a larger space than they needed, in the knowledge that Mr Simmonds would cut their application down to size. 'We must cut the space,' he would say. 'Let them bring their best stuff and leave the worst at home. It can't all be good. Let them bring their best!' Mr Simmonds went on to become Secretary of the Society and make two significant contributions to its progress. Firstly, in laying down procedures for the organisation of both Chelsea and the Westminster Shows and, secondly, in his research and writing of the history of the Society which culminated in his address to its Fellows in 1954 on the 150th anniversary of its founding.

Mr Ron Sargent

Sargent's Lock

33

King George V and Queen Mary inspect a rock garden

Two Chelsea Shows of the 1930s were closely associated with Royal events. In 1935 King George V and Queen Mary celebrated their Silver Jubilee, and in spite of cold, wet weather during the staging period, the exhibitors came up to scratch and the sun shone for the Royal visit. Their Majesties 'were obviously pleased with the wonderful variety of exhibits on view, and with the quiet but warm-hearted homage they received from officials and exhibitors.'

But just a few months later the happiness of the nation in celebrating the Silver Jubilee turned to great sadness, for in January 1936 King George died. The nation was not to have Edward VIII (incidentally a keen and knowledgeable gardener) as King for many months, and after the unsettling effects of the Abdication, the Chelsea Show warmly welcomed King George VI and Queen Elizabeth in 1937, their Coronation Year. Both were known to be garden lovers and, according to the *Gardener's Chronicle*, appeared to thoroughly enjoy their visit. The journal also described the Show's official tribute to the Coronation, the Empire exhibit, 'which illustrated the immense diversity of the vegetation of our Empire on which "the sun never sets." For the first time in the history of the world, one was able to see, under one roof, even though of canvas, plants from the icy Arctic and from the sultry tropics with others from many temperate climes.'

The 1930s were difficult years for the nation, and the Depression had its effect on some of the big estates. Nevertheless, Chelsea continued to be an important social occasion, and there was certainly still a number of wealthy

*King George VI and
Queen Elizabeth — both
great garden lovers*

customers ready to place orders with the exhibitors. The family firm of Strawson were established exhibitors at Chelsea of high quality greenhouses, and Mr R.F. Strawson, who is still a member of the RHS Shows Committee, remembers that in the mid 1930s his father was approached at the Show by a well-dressed gentleman, with bowler hat and umbrella, who wished to have a greenhouse made for his garden at Leatherhead, Surrey. The house was to be black on the outside, with flutings at the corners to be finished in gold leaf. Mr Strawson Senr was sickened and upset. 'We can't associate ourselves with it,' he protested, but eventually overcame his qualms to fill the order, which turned out to be for the owner of a department store that is still well known today.

As if to echo the 'storm clouds gathering over Europe' the weather for the 1939 Chelsea Show was foul, with howling winds and torrential rain that fell relentlessly. The Show itself was generally acknowledged to be outstanding, but it was to be the last for many years, for when war was eventually announced later in the year Chelsea was cancelled until further notice.

Once again, the Royal Horticultural Society worked with a will to inform and educate on the subject of fruit and vegetable production, and co-operated with the Ministry of Information to give lectures and make films. A model allotment was laid out at Wisley and photographs of the work there were used to illustrate the RHS publication, *The Vegetable Garden Displayed*. The book is still available and has sold many thousands of copies.

The 1914-18 war had wrought many changes, but the long and painful years

*Lord Aberconway,
President of the Royal
Horticultural Society
from 1931 to 1953*

from 1939 to 1945 finally overturned the old order of things. Nothing would ever be quite the same again, and nobody had the heart to talk about organising a Chelsea Flower Show. The horticultural trade was nervous and apprehensive. The estate owners, who had long been their customers, no longer had the resources of finance or labour. Who would come? Who would place the large orders to fill their books and make the effort worthwhile? Moreover, stocks of ornamental plants had been depleted with the emphasis on food production and nurserymen asserted that they needed time to replenish.

One man obviously had an instinctive feeling that everything would be all right — the Society's President, Lord Aberconway. Immediately after the war, the Society's funds were badly depleted and costs had risen, but the President refused to inflict restrictions on its activities, and instead took the controversial decision to double subscription fees. Then, in October 1946, amid opposition from Council members, he asserted, 'Whatever else we do without, we should not go without a Chelsea Flower Show next year.'

Lord Aberconway had become President in 1931, when he was the Hon Henry McLaren. He was a politician — a Liberal Member of Parliament and for a while Parliamentary Private Secretary to Lloyd George — and an industrialist, becoming chairman of John Brown & Company, the great shipbuilders who were to produce the 'Queen Mary', 'Queen Elizabeth' and 'Queen Elizabeth II'. The President was also, of course, a great horticulturist, and was charged in about 1903 with the care of the gardens of the family estate at Bodnant in North Wales by his mother, whose own father had originally laid them out. In the ensuing years he planted the gardens — with rhododendrons, azaleas, magnolias and camellias in particular — and collected under glass *Amaryllis, Clivias* and others.

His call for a Chelsea Show in 1947 could not be ignored, and in spite of the protested difficulties, it was a triumph of achievement and a much needed tonic for a bereaved nation. Among the outstanding exhibits was one by the President himself, in association with his gardener, Mr Puddle, consisting of large rhododendrons from Bodnant.

The old order had not entirely disappeared. At one of the first Chelsea Shows after the war, the well-known exhibitor Clarence Elliott had a garden on the Rock Bank, planted in part with *Gentiana acaulis*. Early on the first morning, the very young member of staff on duty on the stand was approached by a well-dressed lady who briskly said, 'I'll have five thousand of those. Send them round to my gardener. Lady Northcliffe. Good Morning.'

However, it gradually became apparent that the new customers for the horticultural trade were not the wealthy few, but the many, many enthusiastic amateurs — ordinary people who wanted to produce 'bloom from the rubble' in the gardens of their detached, semi-detached and terraced houses or 'pre-fabs' and were keen for new plants and information to fuel their hobby.

Just after the war, another hobby associated with horticulture was introduced — the art of flower arranging. In 1947, floral artist and judge Julia Clements (later Lady Seton) travelled on the 'Queen Elizabeth' to the International Flower Show in New York at the same time as Lord Aberconway, who was to be principal guest at the show. There, they were amazed to see flower arrangements in illuminated niches that, she says, 'were surely works of art' and in great contrast to the huge, symmetrical bowls of flowers 'arranged for effect' as the judging rules in Britain had it. Until that time, floral art had been dominated by Constance Spry, who had started a business in the 1930s providing floral decorations for Society parties, dances and dinners in private houses. At Chelsea, customers would select an ornate and expensive vase, which may be filled with flowers by the butler or other member of staff. But in 1948, amateur flower arrangers showed at Chelsea, and a class was introduced that has grown immeasurably in popularity. Julia Clements and other enthusiasts spread the message with effective zeal, and still judge at Chelsea and many other shows.

As well as reflecting social change, the Shows of the post-war years saw exhibits from some outstanding and diverse Chelsea 'regulars' whose reputation survives them. Back in 1931, Mr Eric Savill (later to become Sir Eric) became deputy surveyor of Windsor Parks and Woods and in the next year, selected a site for a small woodland garden, in the Royal Park at Windsor where he proceeded to plant subjects given by Lord Aberconway, Mr Lionel de Rothschild and others. His endeavours were encouraged by members of the Royal Family, particularly King George VI, and the 'Savill Gardens' became renowned for its beautiful woodland setting with many species of rhododendrons and other shrubs. His arrangements at Chelsea, under the auspices of the Crown Estate Commissioners, echoed this appealing, informal woodland style and were immensely popular with visitors.

Harry Wheatcroft was quite simply one of the best known and most popular figures in gardening this century, comparable only with Percy Thrower in his status as a household name, and variously known as 'Mr Rose', 'The King of Roses' and 'The Prince of Rose Growers.' He started growing roses in 1919, together with his brother Alfred, and later moved to Ruddington, Nottingham-shire, from which nursery his firm — as representative of the French Meilland family of rose growers — introduced 'Peace', one of the world's most popular roses, and many more varities including 'Tzigane', 'Queen Elizabeth', 'Super Star' and 'Fragrant Cloud'. That Harry Wheatcroft should introduce 'Peace' to Britain was entirely appropriate, for he was a lifelong pacifist and socialist, and managed to find a great deal of time to give his tremendously popular, witty and entertaining talks and lectures to eager groups of amateur gardeners in clubs and societies throughout the country, as well as travelling extensively abroad in search of new roses.

At the Chelsea Show he was an unmistakable, larger than life figure with his huge moustache, and a unique sartorial style that once earned him the title of one of the 'best dressed men of the year', but prompted the RHS *Journal* to comment, on the introduction of the brilliant red and orange rose named 'Harry Wheatcroft' in 1972, 'We were in fact undecided on the first day whether Mr Harry Wheatcroft has raised a rose to suit his style in sartorial accessories or whether he had dressed for the occasion to match his rose.' He was generous and loved people, and spent many long hours at the Show talking to the constant stream of visitors who pressed around his stand, undecided as to

whether Mr Wheatcroft or his roses held the greater appeal. Although, as his friend Walter Gregory, wrote, his death in 1977 left the world a duller place, his roses survive as his best memorial.

Miss Beatrix Havergal was from an entirely different mould, although equally knowledgeable and enterprising in her specialist horticultural subject. In 1932 she founded the Waterperry Horticultural School for women near Wheatley, Oxford and by the 1950s staged, together with her 'young ladies' of whom she was most protective, regular exhibits of large, luscious strawberries — particularly the variety 'Royal Sovereign'. Her stand was almost invariably awarded a Gold Medal by the Royal Horticultural Society and became a frequent port of call for Royal visitors to the Show, who would, naturally, be offered a strawberry or two to taste. Most did so enthusiastically, but Will Ingwersen remembers a moment of Royal dissent.

As a member of Council, Mr Ingwersen, together with his wife, was conducting the late Duke of Gloucester around the Show, who was of course a very tall man. When the party came to the Waterperry stand, Miss Havergal offered the Duke a strawberry as was her wont, and the Duke turned abruptly to look down at Mrs Ingwersen, about half his own height, and ask, 'D'you like strawberries?' She replied, 'Yes sir, don't you?' 'Spoil the port,' came the gruff reply, and the Duke moved on to the next exhibit.

1951 was the year of the Festival of Britain, and a special effort was made by

Miss Beatrix Havergal offers Princess Margaret a strawberry

OPPOSITE

Harry Wheatcroft, equally famous for his roses and his unique sartorial style

39

exhibitors to make the Chelsea Show a Festival of Flowers — an effort that was judged to have superb results. But the early 1950s were also touched by sadness, for in 1952 the beloved King George VI, who had taken such an interest in Chelsea and all the Society's activities, died. Then in May 1953 came a loss that was much more personal to the Society's members — the untimely death of Lord Aberconway, the President, who is still remembered with respect and affection. Queen Mary, whose attendance at Chelsea had been unfailingly enthusiastic in all weathers, also died in the same year. As the country celebrated the Coronation of the new Queen Elizabeth II, Lord Aberconway was succeeded as President of the Royal Horticultural Society by her uncle, Sir David Bowes-Lyon, younger brother of HRH Queen Elizabeth the Queen Mother.

Sir David had spent some time in his youth working in the Royal Botanic Gardens at Kew, having been prescribed 'open air' activity for the benefit of his health, and so had a good understanding as well as an appreciation of horticulture. He spent a great deal of time working in his own garden at St Paul's Walden Bury, where he carried out much restoration work. Like his predecessor,

The Queen escorted at Chelsea by her uncle, Sir David Bowes-Lyon. Mr Simmonds appears on the extreme right of the picture.

Sir David was a very busy man who nevertheless managed to devote much time and effort to the Society's activities, and, being a person of tremendous charm and sincerity, was greatly loved by everybody from the members of the Royal Family to the office juniors in Vincent Square, as well as by the RHS members.

In the 1960s the nature of the horticultural trade changed yet again in a significant way, with the introduction of garden centres — hitherto an American phenomenon. Russells of Richmond Nurseries, Windlesham, Surrey have exhibited at Chelsea since 1913, and were particularly well known for their stove plants in the 1920s and 30s and for shrubs since 1947.

In a recent lecture to members of the Society, Mr Louis Russell explained that the shrub exhibitors no longer take as many orders at Chelsea for shrubs to be delivered in autumn, both because transport costs are high and because container-grown plants are available throughout the year from garden centres. However, very few offer the new and unusual plants that can still be seen each year at the Chelsea Show.

Other phenomena of the 60s were the many exhibits staged by local authority

Carter's Tested Seeds — still showing vast banks of flowers in the 1950s

41

A rock garden by Gavin Jones Nurseries in 1959

parks departments and the increase in significance of the overseas exhibits, particularly Holland, Belgium and South Africa. Holland and Belgium especially have always maintained close links with Chelsea — links that are valued by the Society.

It is perhaps too soon to assess the decade of the 70s at Chelsea. Certainly it opened with a growing interest in conservation — in plants as in other areas — and produced increasing economic stringencies that make life more difficult for exhibitors. But, like gardening itself, the 'history of Chelsea' is not static and finite, and is seen differently by each pair of eyes that looks over its shoulder at what has gone before. Each season offers new hope, new possibilities, a new opportunity to try and achieve the best yet — an opportunity that is unfailingly and enthusiastically grasped by exhibitors and organisers alike.

CHAPTER 3

I T IS hard to imagine anything with which the organisation of the Chelsea Show today can be compared. Great and well known exhibitions are held in the established centres at Birmingham, Olympia and Earls Court, but these are under cover and have permanent facilities for stands, catering, toilets and so on. Regular visitors to Chelsea know that such facilities are far from permanent at this show, and many wonder at the effort and organisation involved in getting everything ready, only for it all to be removed again just five days later.

To anyone who has never been to Chelsea, how ridiculous it sounds when you attempt to explain that the world's greatest and most famous flower show is held in a public park that, for eleven months of the year, consists solely of grass, trees and roadways, is always open to the elements and, until five days before the Show itself, is also open to the public. If you went on to explain that this flower show is actually run on the same basic lines as the first of its kind to be held on the site in 1912, with many of the same family firms participating, that it is organised by a committee of interested volunteers and a permanent staff of three or four, and that the same committee and staff also organise twelve indoor flower shows in the course of the year, you would surely be greeted with incredulous bewilderment.

Furthermore, your audience would probably imagine that, in these circumstances, the preparations for this show must be chaotic and near disastrous.

On the contrary; panic and disorder have no prominent place at Chelsea, for the Chelsea Show seems to have a life of its own, a capacity for simply happening on the third week in May, every year, and for always appearing 'better than ever' — for the simple reason that the President unfailingly says it is so.

But to give the impression that Chelsea occurs like clockwork would be a mistake, for clockwork is inhuman and mechanical, and Chelsea has nothing to do with mechanics. It does, on the other hand, have everything to do with humanity — with companionship and people's shared feelings of pride and loyalty to a world famous institution, their love of plants and gardens and infinite capacity for discussing them with fellow enthusiasts, even with their aspirations for success and the frustration and exhaustion that must be overcome in order to achieve it. But not just success in a worldly sense; rather the search to meet a challenge, to achieve one's personal best and the lasting respect of one's peers.

Not that the Show is arranged and staged in a rarified atmosphere of constant idyll and cheerful agreement on the part of all concerned — far from it. Human nature sees to it that there are always some complaints, disagreements and grudges; always the machinations of internal politics. But since 1913, exhibitors have been dissatisfied with some of the arrangements, and felt that the organisers fail to appreciate all their problems, and the RHS in its turn has been tempted to wonder impatiently whether it is humanly possible to please everybody.

The organisation of Chelsea is certainly a formidable task. Space must be allocated to exhibitors and some control exercised over their comings and goings. The site, the marquee and all the familiar services and facilities must be arranged, including stands, toilets and plumbing, electricity, telephones, catering, site security and clearance. Finally, everybody must appear in the right place, at the right time and hopefully without mishap or disaster. The method by which the various essential elements are brought together may be steeped in tradition, but the Royal Horticultural Society has evolved an approach whereby traditions are maintained not simply for their own sake, but because they work. When they are seen to work no longer, then they are adapted to suit changing circumstances.

When the marquee was starting to become more crowded each year, and gangways were becoming congested, a one-way system was introduced at the President's suggestion and, in spite of widespread scepticism, it has proved admirably effective. When the chestnut trees in Main Avenue became too large for comfort, the stands were moved backwards by a few feet.

Whilst maintaining its reputation as guardian of the best traditions, the Royal Horticultural Society has therefore shown a surprising capacity for flexibility, which has undoubtedly helped it to survive and grow. After the vicissitudes of its earlier history, the RHS has grown into an organisation that boasts approximately 78,000 members, a formidable establishment at its offices in Westminster, two London exhibition halls, a successful trading and publishing arm and a garden at Wisley whose trainees and research are highly respected among horticultural circles throughout the world.

A show in the Society's New Hall at Westminster

Mr John Mattock —
well known rose grower
and current Chairman of
the Shows Committee

Mr John Cowell,
Secretary of the RHS

The offices and 'Old Hall' stand in Vincent Square — an imposing building that was designed especially for the Society, and officially opened in 1904 by King Edward VII. The glass-roofed hall was described by the King as 'magnificent', but perhaps the most eloquent description of the building and its location appeared in the catalogue for the Chelsea Show of 1914:

'The Society has been exceedingly fortunate both in the site and in the architect. All London might be searched in vain for a better position. It is at once so close to Westminster, and to Victoria Street, and yet it is so absolutely retired, and with such a grand stretch of trees and green grass in front, that at times one might almost fancy the situation to be in the country. Fortunate, too, in the choice of an architect (Mr Edwin Stubbs, of Craven Street, Strand) who, making the very utmost of every inch of the site, has produced a Hall which is the most pleasantly attractive, the lightest, and one of the best acoustically in London — a very handsome and convenient building for all purposes.'

But by 1924, the Old Hall already proved inadequate to meet the Society's needs, and so a nearby site was acquired for a second hall in Greycoat Street, to the rear of Vincent Square. The 'New Hall', as it has been known since its opening in June 1928, is another impressive building with a glass roof, but it is the upper floors of the Old Hall building that have become the centre of power and administration for the Society, which now has quite a complex structure.

Honorary positions are held by the President, and a number of Vice-Presidents, and by members of the Council, which takes major policy decisions. The Society considers itself fortunate in its President, the Lord Aberconway, a man of great charm and formidable intellect, who has worked assiduously on its behalf, and who enjoys enthusiastic support from its members.

As a child of only six or seven, Lord Aberconway remembers helping to stage rhododendrons from Bodnant at Vincent Square for one of the indoor shows. Later, he attended Eton and went on to read Modern Greats and History at Oxford; he was also called to the bar, but has never practised. In the early days of his father's Presidency, he had little involvement with the RHS, for the Council thought that Charles would be his father's 'yes man' — an idea that provoked some mirth among the directors of the engineering company John Brown, where his father was chairman. 'I was already known as always one to ask an awkward question,' he explains.

Lord Aberconway himself has recently retired as chairman of John Brown, but for many years has successfully combined his Presidency of the Society with the great responsibilities of his numerous business interests. He shares his father's horticultural interest in rhododendrons and azaleas — to be found in rare abundance and variety at Bodnant — but is not, he says, a great plantsman, as was his father. As President, he has tried to be more democratic and 'I like to think that I know how to run a meeting, and keep everyone happy and amused.'

One of Lord Aberconway's achievements as a Council member was to introduce junior membership of the Society, as he felt it was vital to encourage the enthusiasm of young people for horticulture. His own son and step-daughter were the first juniors to be enrolled. That son, Michael, is now in his early twenties, has gained a degree in law at Oxford and plans to practise as a barrister. He too is interested in horticulture and is devoted to the gardens at Bodnant.

As for the future of the Society, the President is content with the success of both the Westminster and Chelsea Shows, but would like to increase the staff at the Wisley Gardens, where the number of visitors has risen rapidly to some 400,000 a year, making added demands on those responsible for its upkeep.

At Vincent Square, the Council meets with Lord Aberconway in the imposing Presidential Chair in the second floor Council Room. This quiet, timber-panelled chamber has windows on two sides, mostly overlooking the peaceful green of trees and the playing fields of Westminster School in the Square. Its walls convey an awesome sense of history, with portraits of Sir Joseph Banks and several previous Presidents.

Mr Ian Roger, Halls Superintendent

A great deal of additional voluntary work is carried out by the many experts and enthusiasts who sit on the Society's Committees; all make decisions and recommendations that are referred back to the Council for final approval or amendment. Ten standing committees and eight joint committees pursue the advancement of specific types of plants, and make awards to exhibits, and to individual plants, at the Westminster and Chelsea Shows. Six further committees deal with such matters as the Library, Examinations and — most relevant to Chelsea — the Society's shows. The Shows Committee has a Chairman — Mr John Mattock of the well known Oxfordshire rose growers — and twenty-six members. Membership is by invitation and includes the President and Treasurer, together with the principals of companies whose names, as exhibitors, have been familiar to Chelsea goers for many years — names such as Notcutt, Russell, Slocock, Hillier and Ingwersen. As well as nurserymen, there are representatives of past and current exhibitors of machinery and garden sundries.

These honorary positions are temporary to varying degrees; the Society's considerable salaried staff (thirty-three are employed in administration at Vincent Square alone) is headed by its Secretary, Mr John Cowell.

John Cowell is the son of a foreign office diplomat, who attended Westminster School and gained an MA in History at Cambridge. In 1958, following a spell with the London Chamber of Commerce, he joined the RHS in the subscriptions office. As is customary in the Society's establishment, he made slow, steady progress in promotion from secretary of the Fruit Group to assistant to the assistant Secretary, deputy Secretary, Secretary Designate and, finally, in 1975, Secretary of the Royal Horticultural Society. He is a thoughtful, even tempered man, with a ready sense of wry amusement. 'You could say,' he remarks, 'that administration is in my blood' — a quality that he combines with a fondness for gardening.

Allan Sawyer, Shows Manager, with his assistant in the Shows Office

Among John Cowell's ambitions for the future of the Society is that it should be seen as a national society, orientated to the whole country. One way in which this idea is already being developed is by the touring of lectures given originally at Vincent Square by contemporary experts on horticultural subjects. However, when it comes to Chelsea, he believes, as do the organisers and exhibitors, that the Great Spring Show belongs firmly in the grounds of the Royal Hospital.

In addition to general administration, there are specialist groups of staff such as those responsible for the Halls, under Halls Superintendent Ian Roger. This dour Scot of impeccable appearance is also responsible for the 'nuts and bolts' at Chelsea, overseeing the stand contractors, plumbers and electricians and making his own staff of six available for the installation of accessories such as hessian screens and ropes around the outdoor exhibits.

A number of horticultural experts are employed and in residence at Wisley, under the control of the Garden's Director, Mr Chris Brickell, and the Society's Editor, Elspeth Napier, is responsible for the *Journal*, distributed free to members and now published on behalf of the RHS by an outside firm.

Almost all the Society's committee members and staff become involved with Chelsea in some way, but those who take the central role in staging the Show are the Council, the Shows Committee and the permanent staff of the Shows Office, which is run by Shows Manager Allan Sawyer, with an assistant, a secretary and one part-time assistant.

Allan Sawyer succeeded Ron Sargent in the post in 1978, after a five year grounding in most of the Society's administrative functions, and a period of eighteen months in the role of understudy to his predecessor. As might be expected, he has brought his own approach to the job, and has earned the general respect of exhibitors for his manner of brisk, efficient, yet calm and friendly authority. As Shows Manager, he is readily accessible, and at Chelsea is a familiar figure most often to be seen riding his folding bicycle purposefully around the site, shouting the occasional greeting or response to a passing question. Allan had little interest in gardening before joining the staff of the RHS, but he says it has grown on him, and he is now very much a part of the horticultural scene. 'In this job,' he says, 'you need endless patience and common sense, and a stable temperament. Of course, the need to get on with people goes without saying, but in the gardening world that's not difficult — most of those interested in gardening are nice people.'

Of the twelve indoor shows a year, for which his office is also responsible, the largest and most impressive is the Great Autumn Show, held in both Halls and sometimes regarded as a 'mini Chelsea'. It takes place for three days in the third week of September, and attracts a significant number of the well known Chelsea exhibitors, who have the opportunity of showing plants appropriate to a different season, and of meeting visitors in more intimate surroundings.

Some of the 'fortnightly shows' (as they are still popularly known, although now held at rather less frequent intervals during parts of the year) incorporate competitions held by 'kindred societies' — and a number of specialist societies also stage their own shows in the Halls. They include such bodies as the National Chrysanthemum, British Iris, Alpine Garden and Daffodil Societies, made up of amateur enthusiasts and affiliated to the RHS. Also affiliated are most of the numerous horticultural societies up and down the country. The rules for their local shows and exhibitions are often based on guidelines set by the Society, who offer a Banksian Medal to the exhibitor who wins the highest amount of prize money in a show season. In this way, the influence of the RHS and its own shows is extended to gardeners throughout the British Isles.

The Westminster shows play an important role where Chelsea is concerned, as a proving ground for exhibitors whose capabilities are unknown to the Shows Committee. Potential exhibitors are usually asked to stage a display at several shows, and the responsibility to create a good impression is keenly felt.

On the sundries side, the Committee encourages manufacturers to exhibit their own products, rather than allow a retailer to do so on their behalf, as Chelsea provides a valuable opportunity for the manufacturers to come into direct contact with the gardening public who use their products.

All prospective exhibitors must give details of their proposed exhibit when applying for space, and, where gardens are concerned, a plan and assurance of plant availability must also be submitted. Applications for space are made to the Secretary between September and January, and the Show is always over-subscribed, so that there are inevitably disappointments.

The Society is constantly mindful of its essentially horticultural character. Chelsea is concerned not so much with ordinary plants being shown in a spectacular way — as are many of the Continental extravaganzas — but with the quality and range, often of rare or unusual plants, that Chelsea offers for the enjoyment and information of the horticultural connoisseur and novice alike. This is not just an invitation to gape, but an opportunity for enrichment and inspiration for those truly interested in plants and gardens.

A delightful quirk that typifies both the tradition and the practical approach to the organisation of Chelsea, is that prospective exhibitors of gardens in the open are sent, with their application forms, a copy of the previous year's *Show Schedule*, containing all the relevant rules and regulations. However, this is no cause for confusion, for the simple reason that the *Schedule* does not discernibly differ from year to year.

A further characteristic quirk is that all the rules — which in the main were shaped by Mr Simmonds during his service in the Shows Office — are entirely at the Secretary's discretion. Although the rules are normally adhered to, it is therefore possible for unusual exhibits to be accommodated, if they are felt to be an asset to the Show as a whole.

By the same token, Mr Simmonds was known to exercise his discretion in the opposite direction — by finding the means to outlaw an exhibitor's activities. In the 1950s Mr Ambrose Congreve — a flamboyant character by all accounts — exhibited a rock garden and, on Press day, employed scantily clad young ladies to pose for the photographers, sitting on the rocks. This would not do at all for Mr Simmonds, who gathered the Shows Committee around him to discuss the grounds upon which action could be taken. He eventually came up with reference to Paragraph 30 of the *Schedule*, which is headed 'Articles not allowed'. Included in a list of items which 'May not be exhibited or used in any part of the Show' is 'livestock of any kind (except with the special permission of the Secretary)' — a rule that had been introduced following the inclusion, for some unaccountable reason, of a group of goats on a garden exhibited in a previous year. The models were triumphantly categorised as livestock, and as such were required to be removed, the Secretary, in this instance, being in no mood to give his special permission!

The same paragraph reflects the strictly horticultural nature of the Show, for other articles not allowed include 'Artificial plants, flowers, foliage, fruit or vegetables; bunches of cut flowers . . . highly coloured figures including animals, birds, gnomes, fairies or any similar creatures, actual or mythical, for use as garden ornaments.'

When all applications for space have been received and vetted, the Shows Manager drafts a plan for the layout of the actual site, and the interior of the marquee, accommodating all the proposed exhibitors, although it may be necessary to reduce slightly the amount of space they have requested. This plan is put before the Shows Committee for discussion and final decisions a week before the Society's annual general meeting in February. The final decision on space for exhibitors is taken at this meeting, and is the only decision that is reported, rather than referred, by a committee to the Council, the finalised plans being put before the Council at a brief meeting held just before the AGM.

On the Thursday morning of the Show itself, a serious check on exhibitors is carried out, when selected members of the Shows Committee divide into two groups of six — known with some dread among exhibitors as the 'Thursday committees' — and an inspection is made to assess the quality of stands and see that the rules are being adhered to. This particularly applies to the trade stands, where trading methods and integrity are as important as standards of display. Concern about shortcomings and transgressions and, in some cases, stern warnings, are conveyed to the hapless exhibitor by letter shortly after the Show.

Inevitably, the Society receives some complaints from visitors after the Show, and those concerning exhibitors are dealt with by Peter Salter, one of the assistant Secretaries. The majority concern non-delivery of goods — most often found to be due to success on the part of a small company on a scale with which it simply cannot cope. Comment is also invited from exhibitors; the points they raise are always discussed by the Council, and often acted upon.

The organisation of exhibitors is vital, but there would be no show at which to exhibit if meticulous arrangements were not made to secure the availability of the site, and all the facilities and services associated with, and essential to Chelsea. As far as the site is concerned, the arrangement with the Royal Hospital for the use of its South Grounds is unique, for in spite of a number of requests, the space is not made available for any other exhibition.

Anybody who has ever been to Chelsea will also appreciate that the beautiful, symmetrical form of the Hospital building, with its spacious, terraced lawns overlooked by large cannon, conveys a sense of history and atmosphere that pervades the site. The Hospital was founded by King Charles II in 1682, built by Sir Christopher Wren and completed in 1692. It is still used for its original purpose, as a home for old soldiers. King Charles had re-established a standing army in Britain in 1660, and some twenty years later became aware of the need for a home for its veterans. The concept of a hostel was undoubtedly inspired not by the influence of Nell Gwynn, as one story goes, but by the founding, by Louis XIV, of Les Invalides in Paris. But the finance for running such an establishment in London proved a problem. This was eventually volunteered by Sir Stephen Fox, the Paymaster General.

The Hospital is now controlled by a board of commissioners, and the Paymaster General of the day still holds the post of senior commissioner. It was built to accommodate 450 men, but as the army increased in size, the Hospital became inadequate even before its completion, and so an army pension was introduced, its recipients being known as 'out-pensioners'. There are now some 440 in-pensioners, most aged sixty-five or over. No fewer than 100 are veterans of the First World War, and there is one remaining veteran of the Boer War. Qualifications for admission are 'good character' and freedom from family encumbrances.

Although the Hospital is still run on military lines, its residents enjoy a good deal of freedom and receive numerous invitations to attend functions ranging from state occasions and regimental reunions to Wimbledon, or even a day by the sea in Brighton, by courtesy of the London taxi drivers. The Chelsea Show is one event to which these old gentlemen need no invitation, for they have free access during its preparation and staging, and most seem to enjoy thoroughly this break from routine. The Hospital has space devoted to allotments, and those keen gardeners among its residents relish the opportunity for a chat with fellow enthusiasts, and a chance to reminisce. Even those with no interest in gardening make the most of this captive audience for their jokes and stories!

One pensioner, Mr Gibbs, keeps bees in the allotment area, and the honey they produce became, on one occasion, the subject of a Royal incident. During the celebrations for the Queen's Silver Jubilee, the Prince of Wales attended the

A Chelsea Pensioner holds his audience captive!

51

Founder's Day dinner at the Hospital, and among the residents to whom he was introduced was Gibbs. On being told that Gibbs kept bees, the Prince replied, 'Oh, I'm very fond of honey. Perhaps you could spare me a pot?' 'No, certainly not,' retorted Gibbs, 'I have far too many customers.' Later, the Governor apologised to the Prince on Gibbs' behalf, saying he was sure Gibbs had misheard. The Prince, however, was certain Gibbs had not, and was highly amused by the incident. When Gibbs was next bottling honey from his bees, he was sent for by the Adjutant, and duly despatched to Buckingham Palace by taxi to deliver, in person, two jars of honey to Prince Charles. Ever since, he is regularly asked by fellow residents, with a grin, whether he now labels his jars 'By Royal Appointment'.

The land belonging to the Hospital extends to some seventy acres, from Tite Street to Chelsea Bridge Road and from Royal Hospital Road to the Chelsea Embankment. Ranelagh Gardens lays to one side, bordering Chelsea Bridge Road (opposite Chelsea Barracks) and the Embankment, and is open to the public. To its west is the central part of the South Grounds, where the Chelsea Show is held. For 325 days of the year, this area is leased to the Royal Borough of Kensington and Chelsea, and it too is open as a public park.

But for forty days, from midnight of the last Monday in April, the South Grounds are on leasehold rental to the Royal Horticultural Society. The lease agreement is for a ten year period, with provision for a review after five years, and under its terms the Society is responsible for drainage, roads, water supply and some of the electrical points, as well as care and restoration of the site. Ranelagh Gardens is also made available, but only for the purpose of catering and toilet facilities. Further terms of the lease make allowance for respecting the peace and quiet of the Hospital; for instance, during staging of the Show, no noisy work may be carried out between 10 pm and 7 am.

The grounds are effectively taken over by the RHS on the Tuesday of the last week in April — which also happens to coincide with the first day of a Rhododendron show at Vincent Square. On this day, a pre-Show inspection of the entire site is carried out by the Society's Secretary and Shows Manager and the Hospital's Secretary and Governor, accompanied by Mr Taylor, an ex-local authority Parks Superintendent, who acts as an independent assessor. The five men walk the entire site to consider its state of repair. This is the end of the football season, so note is taken of areas of grass well covered and areas that are worn; any tree or shrub with damage is noted; every cracked kerbstone is recorded.

When this meeting takes place, the end of the forty-day period seems a lifetime away, for it will be forty days of intense activity, during which heavy lorries carrying fragile blooms or stately trees will undoubtedly crack or dislodge kerbstones; the caterer's lorry will probably drive over the grass in Ranelagh Gardens, and may even demolish a drystone wall; garden exhibitors will excavate for footings, ponds and plant beds and, it being the British summer, the heavens may open. But at the end of it all, in forty days' time, another tour of inspection will take place with the same five people in attendance. The exhibitors will have reinstated their own sites, the rock bank will have been renovated and reseeded and the Society's own staff from Wisley will have repruned the shrubs, reseeded the turf and rebuilt any demolished walls in Ranelagh Gardens.

Nevertheless, the Hospital's own grounds staff will still have restoration work to do, and the purpose of the meeting will be to agree on a reasonable sum that the Society must pay the Hospital to complete the restoration of the grounds, so that football and tennis can once again be played, and children and dogs can once again be taken for quiet walks.

By and large, the arrangements with the Royal Hospital are amicable, and its staff feel that they have little cause for concern while the Show is in progress, for they know everything will be put back just as the RHS found it. There are incidental benefits, too. After the Show, the Hospital's garden yard is full of bounty bestowed upon it by generous exhibitors, as well as individual gifts of plants made to some of the more horticulturally-minded residents.

During the Show, the Hospital has two marquees in Ranelagh Gardens, close to the Hospital entrance. Here, visitors can buy from residents craft goods made by them and mementoes ranging from a printed tea towel to a plaster model of a pensioner wearing the familiar red coat of his 'Number One' uniform. Also

The Chillianwallah Monument

during the Show, a charity collection is made which was, until recently, in aid of local Rotary Clubs' activities. However, the Army Benevolent Fund has now taken over as beneficiary and their collection is, of course, assisted by some of the Chelsea pensioners. In 1981 no less than £11,000 was collected, with one rather handsome, white-haired old gentleman singlehandedly collecting £1,200.

The Hospital administration also benefits from income derived by the sale of parking permits to exhibitors, to allow them to park in front of the Hospital building when the Show is open to the public, and control of parking traffic is another task executed with relish by the residents. Members of the RHS council enjoy the privilege of parking in Light Horse Court, within the confines of the Hospital itself.

One of the most prominent features of the South Grounds is the Chillianwallah Monument. This large obelisk stands in a central position, and was erected by the Royal Welch Fusiliers to commemorate their battle against the Sikhs at Chillianwallah, India — a battle which carries the dubious distinction of being the first at which shells producing shrapnel were used.

The Monument is always at the centre of a marquee exhibit, but creates quite a challenge for exhibitors, because its base and surround are not square with the roads and gangways, being a few inches out all round, and the ground itself is far from level. Perhaps because of the difficulties it presents, the Monument site has come to be recognised as the most prestigious of all marquee exhibits.

Having taken on such importance as an obstacle that must be accommodated by exhibitors, they have always thought of the Monument as being of equal significance to the Hospital — otherwise, why would it be there? It comes as quite a surprise to discover that, according to the Hospital's assistant Secretary, because this is a Regimental monument, it has no place in the Hospital's grounds. Moreover, its speedy removal to the Regiment's headquarters would give great pleasure, if only funds would permit such a feat!

It is not exhibitors alone who are obliged to contend with the Chillianwallah Monument, for the Great Marquee itself must be erected around the edifice. The contract for erecting the largest marquee in the world (a claim authenticated by the *Guinness Book of Records*) has been held by Piggott Bros and Co Limited of Ongar, Essex since 1912, and like almost every other feature of Chelsea, the company has quite a history.

Thomas Courtney was an ex-officer in the British Army who, in 1780, set up a business in the City of London supplying uniforms and tentage. He obtained several army contracts, and soon built up a substantial business, with a branch in Scotland. On his death, in the 1830s, the firm was taken over by his son-in-law, a Mr Piggott. The firm continued to grow, and to supply an ever-increasing range of goods, including footballs, harness and saddlery, banners, street decorations and lanterns, as well as tents for every kind of use. Piggotts are even on record as having supplied tentage to both the opposing armies in the American Civil War. This pioneering spirit was once again displayed when Piggotts made and fitted the fabric coverings to the wings and fuselage of some of the earliest aircraft, and even constructed entire aircraft hangars in canvas. Now, this family firm still concentrates on the original fundamentals of its

Erecting the biggest marquee in the world

*Constructing the stands
in Eastern Avenue*

business: canvas, tentage and flags, and its managing director, Mr Ian Petrie, is himself son-in-law of a Mr Piggott.

Mr Petrie is a jovial, unassuming man, who enjoys Chelsea and, being also a great Royalist, values his connections with the Show. 'We've done the Chelsea marquee so may times,' he says, 'that we don't worry about it any more. It's often less trouble than a small, one-off marquee in somebody's back garden — and we've been lucky in not having any particular problems. The last real blow-down was in the 1920s.'

During the Show, many visitors are a bit alarmed by the sometimes quite loud creaking sounds to be heard in the marquee, but Mr Petrie calmly dismisses their fears. 'It's got to creak a bit. You know what they say — a creaking ship never sinks.' As an afterthought, he admits that when he tours the Show with his wife, she looks at the flowers while he looks up anxiously at the marquee.

Since 1947, the basic area of the marquee has been just under three-and-a-half acres, but there are drainage facilities for it to be extended by up to ninety feet, in ten foot wide bays. Piggotts start work on the erection of the marquee on the last Wednesday in April — the day after the RHS takes over the site, and it takes just over two weeks for twenty-two men to complete the job.

The first task is to prod the ground in one corner with an iron rod, until it hits metal — the first drain. These receive the rectangular wall poles, which are hollow and lined with aluminium. Rainwater drains through the poles, and into

the main underground drains leading away to the River Thames. In case of really heavy rain, an electric pump situated on the west side of the marquee, opposite the ladies' toilets, boosts surplus water into the main drainage system.

Inside the marquee, good light is essential for visitors to see flowers in their true colours and to their best advantage. Photographers and cameramen may complain that the light is too blue or too yellow at times, but if perfection is not achieved, it is not for want of trying. The canvas used at Chelsea is of a particularly fine quality, to let in the maximum amount of light, and is unproofed, as proofing would darken it, and wax proofing also picks up dirt. Being unproofed, it is, however, more susceptible to mildew, and must therefore be reasonably dry before it can be dismantled and stored — a fact that can delay clearance by several days if there is rain at the end of the Show. In a good year, the marquee takes just four days to dismantle; the canvas is stored and then overhauled during January ready for the following April.

Piggotts' hire department used to use part of the canvas for the Chelsea marquee at Southport and other flower shows, but some eight years ago, when the price of canvas started to increase rapidly, the company entered into an arrangement with the RHS whereby the Society has purchased canvas for Piggotts to use exclusively at Chelsea over a ten year period, although both parties hope that the bonus of a couple of years' extra use may be gained.

As the massive marquee posts are hauled into position, the shouts and heaves of the burly workmen are accompanied by the rhythmic sound of hammers and saws from builders and carpenters constructing the timber stands that line Northern and Eastern Avenues. Each open-fronted 'shop' will house an exhibitor of garden sundries, machinery or equipment, books and even floral art, and each must be individually constructed, and painted.

Plumbing and electricity must be installed virtually from scratch, and toilets must be provided not only for exhibitors, but also for the Show's 250,000 or so visitors. In the case of the ladies' toilets, the provisions are perhaps never quite adequate, for — along with refreshments — the subject of the ladies' toilets at Chelsea is one that comes in for perennial discussion, complaint and suggestion.

The lavatory fittings belong to the RHS and are brought out and installed by the Show's official plumber each year, being housed in marquees in Main Avenue and Ranelagh Gardens. During the Show there are always queues, and even the installation does not always go without a hitch. Ron Sargent remembers that one year in the late 1940s, there was a blockage between the toilets in Main Avenue and the main sewer. The ubiquitous Simmonds, as Show Secretary of the day, refused to leave the site until the cause was found and removed. Mr Sargent was despatched to Vincent Square to fetch plans, and an entire exhibitor's stand was taken up before some offending crumbling brickwork was found. The staff were eventually allowed to leave at three o'clock in the morning, with a last reminder to report for that day's duty at 8 am sharp.

Copious quantities of water are needed to keep plants and lawns fresh, and to fill ponds. Taps — again, the same taps each year — are installed to the rear of the outdoor gardens, and in the marquee. Other essential users of water are the caterers, who operate on the basis of a three-year contract. At the time of

The official lavatory fittings

'Angels'

renewal, there is no shortage of catering firms willing to take on the concession. During the build-up period, a marquee houses the ground staff canteen, where sausage and bacon sandwiches, paper cups of tea and the like can be purchased by everybody working on site, including exhibitors.

Just before the Show, the catering staff are obliged to transfer their portable gas ring, tea urn and supplies of sausages to a new location, and the full contingent of some 3,500 exhibitors are obliged to consume rather more sophisticated and expensive food in the official exhibitors' catering marquee in Ranelagh Gardens. One consolation here is the availability of alcoholic beverages — particularly welcome on the chill, damp days that Chelsea is so well capable of producing. On the very hot sunny days that are equally likely, the daisy-studded grass banks of Ranelagh Gardens almost take on the atmosphere of a seaside bank holiday, as exhibitors picnic and sunbathe, enjoying a welcome break from the rigours of duty on their stands.

Meanwhile, in the Show itself, three catering tents offer sustenance to visitors. A bar, and self service snacks and lunches are the order of the day. No longer do the fondly-remembered Lyons 'nippies' wait at table to serve you a three course meal for 5s, as they did in the old days. Gone, too, are the hot dog and hamburger wagons that used to frequent some of the Avenues — banished at the instigation of exhibitors, who complained about the smells. Nowadays, the only mobile concession at Chelsea is for the sale of ice cream — and this only from hand carts rather than vans.

Not only the bodily need for refreshment is catered for; in case of accident or illness the faithful, voluntary staff of St John Ambulance are always in attendance in a small marquee containing wheelchairs, a comprehensive range of medications and first aid equipment. Complaints are usually of a minor nature — visitors feeling faint, or suffering from swollen ankles or headaches. Occasionally, a more dramatic incident may occur, such as the case of the gentleman who suffered a coronary, but returned the following year to make a generous donation in thanks for the actions of the staff, who saved his life.

Each year, as the site is taken over and contractors and exhibitors start to move in, it is the fervent hope of John Cowell, Allan Sawyer and John Mattock that dramatic incidents will be mercifully few and far between.

CHAPTER 4

THE CHELSEA SHOW is a highpoint of the year, not only for the Royal Horticultural Society, but also for hundreds of exhibitors and their staff, who must plan, grow, build, plant and finally explain themselves to an expectant public. There can hardly be a single exhibitor who would not admit that this Show is one of the most important events in their working year — if not the most important. For some, as well as being the biggest and best, it marks the start of a season of shows around the British Isles. For others, it is a unique opportunity to exhibit in distinguished horticultural company, where one's work, plants or goods will be seen by hundreds and thousands of visitors, many of them extremely discerning and well-informed, and possibly — through reports in newspapers and magazines, on radio and television — to many more people besides.

Such exposure at a supremely prestigious event places a tremendous responsibility upon exhibitors to rise to the occasion, and to show the best of which they are capable. There is only one chance each year, and what is done may linger in the memory of visitors, fellow exhibitors — and even the RHS committees — for a long twelve months.

It is probably this desire to do better each year that makes the Show itself the best source of inspiration. Go to Chelsea and ask almost any exhibitor when they start to plan for next year, and the reply will probably be, 'Right now.' Certainly this is true of ourselves, as garden exhibitors — and it is essential, for our application for space must be sent to the RHS in late September, together with an explanation of the theme and purpose of the garden, and details of the design, and features and plants to be included.

In the economic climate before, and even shortly after, the Second World War, gardens at Chelsea were exhibited by designers and landscape companies, relying on their own resources and finance. But exhibiting a garden is now a costly business, and not only is sponsorship in some form almost inevitable, but the nature of garden exhibitors has changed a good deal. Now, they are as likely to be a gardening magazine, a national newspaper (the *Daily Express* is a veteran, and has recently been joined by the *Sunday Times*) or even a large company such as F W Woolworth, promoting its stores' gardening departments.

The gardens themselves also reflect the changing times. No longer are they massive extravaganzas, to be sold and reproduced for a wealthy client with an army of gardeners, but smaller, practical designs to suit the needs and pocket of ordinary homeowners who take an interest in their garden. Often, too, their character reflects modern landscaping trends or current interests, such as vegetable-growing or wild plant conservation.

Exhibitors are allowed to commence work on the outside gardens, on the Rock Bank and in Main Avenue, on the first Friday in May, and by the time that date approaches we will have built up a plump file of correspondence, ordering, requesting and checking such items as materials and plants, leaflets and signboards, tickets and passes, electricity and water supplies and probably one or two rubbish containers, so that when the Show closes the results of these months of work can be dismantled and unceremoniously carted away. But before the Show starts, we have just sixteen days, including weekends and one bank holiday, in which to transform a patch of grass into a complete garden that looks instantly mature.

After restless nights punctuated with dreams of arriving to find no space allocated, of being still unfinished when the Queen arrives, or of the site being covered in a foot of snow, the great day dawns, and with it return the familiar feelings of tension, anxiety, excitement and determination — feelings that mean the start of another Chelsea. By tradition, the first day on site is something of a social reunion, for many of the same people work on the gardens and trade stands, the site works and plumbing, and even the telephones, each year. For the time being, the only telephones are located in the commissionaires' caravan beside the gates at the entrance from Chelsea Embankment; this semi-circular lay-by is known as the 'Bull Ring' and is the only vehicular entrance. The two commissionaires themselves are another essential feature of Chelsea, and usually find time, between opening and closing the gates and answering enquiries for a cup of tea and a chat — even for the occasional piece of Chelsea Show gossip.

During the first few days, the Royal Hospital grounds are comparatively quiet. The occasional vehicle enters or leaves; local residents stroll past, sometimes — but not often — pausing to see what we are doing; Hospital pensioners are more inclined to stop for a chat and tell us, as they do each year, that they can't play football now we're digging up their grass. One pensioner even takes a slow, sedate look around the site from the saddle of a tricycle.

The familiar sight of Allan Sawyer touring the grounds on his bike

A rock garden takes shape

Allan Sawyer is also travelling the site on his bike; Piggotts' men are going through their annual routine in erecting the framework for the marquee, and the stand fitters take their work at a steady, unhurried pace. When it rains, and a chill wind blows from the River Thames, everybody can feel quite wretched, but whatever the weather there is a sense of camaraderie, and on pleasant sunny days a relaxed, cheerful — almost holiday — atmosphere, for this is simply an enjoyable place to work. The work is even accompanied by rousing band music, as on the nearby parade ground of Chelsea Barracks, rehearsals for the annual ceremony of Trooping the Colour are in progress, and the same tunes are repeated over and over again!

All that is to be seen of what will become our garden is a series of small wooden pegs banged into the ground. Allan Sawyer and his staff will have spent some time measuring and marking out the outdoor and marquee stands, and it is only occasionally that a mishap occurs, such as the year when an exhibitor started building his garden in the adjacent plot, then had to recommence in the right place. If a disaster should occur, offers of help are usually forthcoming. Fortunately, disasters are few and far between, although there was the occasion when a section of walling simply blew over, or when our neighbours excavated for a swimming pool too close to the foundations of our six foot high wall, which wobbled threateningly throughout the Show.

Pensioners ponder over the annual transformation

The construction techniques for a garden that must look instantly mature and permanent, but in reality only last five days, inevitably involve some cheating. A fairly weak cement mortar mix is used for building the walls, and the paving is just laid on sand. Sometimes a concrete pool is made, but usually a plastic liner is installed. It is in the planting that most cheating probably occurs. Plants are always the biggest worry, and it is necessary to have grown on something like twice the number that are likely to be used. Which flowers will be at their peak, or will have attained sufficient size, is entirely dependent on the weather, and we can only keep our fingers crossed. The plants can be taken in and out of the greenhouse in response to conditions, but there are bound to be some failures and disappointments.

All the plants are grown and transported in containers, and most — particularly larger shrubs and trees — remain in them, being plunged into the ground, and their containers buried out of sight. This can be a backbreaking task, for whatever the weather during the previous few weeks, the ground is always very hard. Vegetable plants are grown in long wooden boxes, and they, too, are plunged into the ground, producing an instant vegetable plot with immaculately straight lines of thriving crops.

When plants have been positioned and repositioned, their arrangements discussed and argued over, and finally settled, then the soil in all the planted

Plots side-by-side in Main Avenue. Within a matter of days they will look like mature gardens

The deceptively casual early stages of putting up an exhibit before the last-minute frenzy sets in

The Royal Hospital. The setting for more than sixty Chelsea Shows

A rock garden shown by Paul Temple in 1981

Opposite
An unmistakable
production from the
National Farmers
Union

Above left
A spectacular exhibit by
the National Association
of Flower Arranging
Societies

Above right
An American-style
garden on the Rock
Bank by the students of
Merrist Wood College

Left
Adrian Slack with his
carnivorous plants

Bonsai trees — an increasingly popular feature at Chelsea

*Opposite
Prince Philip makes a closer inspection*

Roses — a traditional favourite

A dramatic exhibit of geraniums dominated by a huge swan, shown by the Central Royal Parks and awarded the Society's Lawrence Medal

Opposite
Exotic cacti and succulent plants are a constant source of fascination for visitors

Perfect houseplants displayed with typical flair by the House of Rochford

KALANCHOE
SCHUMACHERI

Colourful annuals forced into glorious perfection for Chelsea areas is covered with a sprinkling of rich, dark brown peat or shredded bark to conceal pots and provide an attractive background for flowers and foliage. If there is a lawn, we pray for dry weather during the Show, so that the grass will not need cutting, for it is best not walked upon at all, and the blades of grass may even be lightly brushed to perfection each morning with a soft broom.

During the second week of preparation, more people and traffic start to appear. The gardens are taking shape, and work begins on some of the outdoor trade stands — building walls, ponds and swimming pools; erecting greenhouses and conservatories and planting trees and shrubs in the nursery exhibits.

Allan Sawyer's office transfers to a tiny portable building perched on a grass bank close to the Embankment entrance. The poles and ropes of the open marquee framework are gradually covered in canvas, like the rigging of a stately ship being prepared to set sail. Inside, the grass is littered with timber trestles and staging, used in greater numbers since digging in the marquee was banned after the Second World War.

Essential equipment

It is strange to think that these ordinary, pedestrian objects, familiar to every church and village hall, will soon perform a quite extraordinary function. Covered and disguised, they will serve as a base for displays of luscious, scarlet strawberries, brilliantly-coloured begonias and delicate clematis the size of saucers, delphiniums as tall as young trees and laden with bloom, waxen, lime-green orchids, fuchsias falling like rain, purple and pink carnations, sweetly scented roses in profusion . . . . very soon, they will all start to arrive.

By Thursday of the second week, preparations approach top gear. From today, the grounds are closed to the public and every exhibitor must have an official pass in order to enter. For vehicles, a one-way system is in operation, which for us means a tour around the perimeter of the marquee in order to reach the gardens. Hold-ups are inevitable, and it is so frustrating to know that the very plants we are waiting to use are stuck in a lorry just a few hundred feet away on the other side of the marquee!

The two commissionaires are joined by numerous uniformed security staff, who are employed by the RHS to stand guard at every entrance and exit, day and night, throughout the Show, and occasionally by individual exhibitors to guard rare and valuable plants. By Sunday, the commissionaires themselves will be pushing a handcart containing their kettle, and other necessities of life, as they move to their post for the rest of the Show — on duty at the entrance to the Society's office in Main Avenue.

For the marquee exhibitors, the major concern is their plants, over which they have worried like sickly babes for the last few weeks and months. Nevertheless, there is usually time to install the portable cooker or gas ring before unloading the lorry. Duly refreshed, they start their impression of characters from the climax of *Macbeth*, as 'Great Birnam wood to high Dunsinane Hill / Shall come.' Vast trees and shrubs with huge root balls; prickly cacti in pots; enormous greenhouse plants; trays of tiny violas and alpines; cut blooms packed in boxes — all must be carried or wheeled on carts, barrows and trolleys to the place where they are needed, and if that is at the centre of the marquee, it can be quite a journey.

A humble wooden bridge is brought into position and becomes the focal point of an exhibit

As among the garden exhibitors, a friendly, club-like atmosphere exists, although there is less time to chat, since the staging period is shorter and more intense, and every exhibitor is conscious that there is a lot of work to be done. For the growers, too, this is the culmination of a long period of careful, meticulous preparation, for at Chelsea it is quality that counts, and poor quality plants can never be compensated for by gimmicks or tricks of display.

The preparation varies in its nature according to the many different types of plants that are shown. Nurseries who exhibit groups of mixed trees and shrubs meet a big challenge — that of bringing to perfection in late May not only seasonal subjects, but plants that would normally bloom in March or April, July or August.

Hillier Nurseries, L.R. Russell and Notcutts Nurseries are well known to visitors for this type of exhibit. All have been showing for many years, and have a succession of Gold Medals to their credit. In the past, the large, family nurseries relied solely on mail order trade from Chelsea, but now customers are just as likely to walk into one of their garden centres and ask for a plant seen on the stand at Chelsea, perhaps nine months previously.

In the early days, shrubs were grown for Chelsea in half-barrels and tubs of daunting weight, and a hernia was acknowledged by workers as an occupational hazard! Now, although modern, lightweight containers — usually plastic — are used, growing is still a time-consuming business. As a rule of thumb, Notcutts will prepare three times as many plants as will eventually appear on their stand, for a third will be past its best by Chelsea week, a third not yet ready and a vital third, just at its peak.

Notcutts' specialist show growers see the whole process as resembling a juggling act. Summer shrubs that are to be forced into early flower are arrayed in greenhouses, but a very warm spell could scorch them, so they are moved out of the house to a cooler, but sheltered position, and if the weather turns suddenly colder, they must all be rushed back inside again. An even greater number of plants — cherries and lilac in particular — are held back from their normal spring flowering season. The plants are put in cold store in January, before the blossoms are even in bud. In April, it is safe to bring them out and allow them to bud and flower in the normal way. But whilst the shrub growers do show many seasonal plants — particularly the traditional rhododendrons and azaleas — in their immense, colourful displays, other exhibitors specialise entirely in flowers that are quite unseasonal, and have no business being in bloom in the third week of May. One of the most dramatic, and easily recognisable, is the daffodil.

Michael Jefferson-Brown has been showing at Chelsea for over ten years, and reckons to have honed to a fine art the business of showing daffodils and narcissi out of season. He modestly claims that it really is devastatingly simple. In February, he goes out into the field, and picks some stems of each variety when it is at its best — a total of about 10,000 flowers. All are placed in buckets of water and put into cold store at a temperature of one degree above freezing point, until one day before the Show. Just before lunchtime on the Sunday of Chelsea week, the daffodils are loaded on to the van and, on arrival in the marquee, some 2,000 blooms are staged in the minimum possible time — a matter of some calculation. A few of the blooms will even stay fresh all week, but most will have to be replaced with spare supplies during the Show.

Of course, as this is Chelsea, these are not only common or garden daffodils, but flowers that are white and pink, vivid orange or soft tangerine, as well as the popular doubles, including 'Unique' — a huge double white and yellow that has received the RHS Award of Merit. Bulbs ranging in price from ten pence to about £40 each can be ordered, and as a result of Chelsea, consignments have been sent to such diverse customers as HM The Queen Mother and a Botanic Garden in Russia.

Other flowers, closely associated with an English summer, must be forced into bloom at just the right moment in well-heated greenhouses — roses, annuals grown from seed, delphiniums, stocks and many more. The dread of exhibitors of these plants is a sudden cold snap, for, once out of their protected environment, they are particularly delicate and susceptible to the shock of an icy draught.

Not only flowers are shown out of season at Chelsea. In recent years, one of the most intriguing attractions in the marquee has been the mature tomato plants, with great clusters of ripe fruit, grown by Fisons in growing bags, and shown at a time when most gardeners are just starting, rather than picking, their crop. The plants are grown at Fisons Levington research station, near Ipswich, from seeds sown at Christmas time. Grower Brian Tree sees that the young plants are provided with both artificial light and heat, and undertakes methodical 'truss tickling' to pollinate the flowers, for it is particularly difficult to set fruit on the lower trusses of the plants at a time of year when natural daylight is abysmal.

Mr Reuthe, whose family showed rhododendrons at the very first Chelsea Show, at lunch amidst his plants

When the tomatoes are ready for packing and transporting to London, a small army of ladies moves in to tie up each bunch of fruit individually in a fibre cleaning cloth, for the fruit is soft from the greenhouse, and can easily be jolted from the plant. On arrival, not only does it take a long time to untie the thousands of cloths, but other, unforeseen problems can occur, such as the greedy blackbirds who fly into the marquee in the evening and, if allowed, feast on the ripe, juicy tomatoes. As the staging progresses, the birds realise that they have hit a winning streak, for there is little that Fisons' staff can do to protect a tomato plant perched high in the air, at the pinnacle of the display!

Gradually, carpets and mountains of flowers and plants take shape, and the billowing canvas of this huge tent gives shelter to a veritable Noah's Ark of the world of cultivated plants. Carnations, cacti and chrysanthemums; paeonies, lilies and pelargoniums; acers, azaleas, conifers and rhododendrons; poppies, ivies, roses, orchids; polyanthus, schizanthus and alstroemerias; hostas and stocks; marigolds, bromeliads and ferns; herbaceous, carnivorous, bulbous, perennial, alpine and annual plants — evocative names that originate from all over the world.

Visitors will be reminded of the bravery and dedication of the early plant-hunting pioneers, informed of the continuing advances of modern plant breeders and delighted by exhibits of native species brought from Colombia, Kenya and

South Africa, as well as displays of superb indoor plants from Belgium and Holland.

The best known exhibitor of indoor plants is undoubtedly the House of Rochford, a company that has expanded dramatically in the last thirty-five years under the direction of Mr T. Rochford, a well-respected Vice-President of the RHS. His wife, Betty, orchestrates the ambitious Chelsea exhibits — exhibits where the plants are veritable Goliaths to the Davids gracing the average suburban window-sill — and more recently has been ably assisted by Mr Jock Davidson and her son, Thomas, who is now the company's managing director.

For the time being, the splendour and magnitude of the whole are far from the thoughts of exhibitors, whose efforts are concentrated on the practicalities of the one small part for which they alone are responsible. In a smaller marquee, an abundance of floral arrangements is prepared by leading amateur exponents of the art, whilst over in Main-Way, at the top of Main Avenue, nimble-fingered professional florists select, snip and stage their choicest blooms.

Among them, working quietly and industriously behind a canvas night screen, with dust sheets on the floor, is Harold Piercey, who is today responsible for keeping alive the great name of Constance Spry. Just a week before, he will have collected his material together, and arrives with his selection of flowers early on Monday morning. All will have been chosen to look as natural as possible — like garden flowers rather than typical florists flowers — and all will conform to a distinct colour theme. This theme is even reflected during the Show in Mr Piercey's choice of shirt and floral Liberty tie. He delights in the

The whole family takes a well-earned break

moment when, during a 'pink' show, he emerged from a much needed tea break backstage, coincidentally clutching a pink wafer biscuit, to hear an American visitor remark to her companion, 'Gee, even the cookies match.'

As well as its horticultural authority, it is the wide range of exhibits that makes Chelsea unique, and machinery, equipment, furniture, tools, chemicals and numerous sundries are as essential — if, apparently, less glamorous — a feature as the excitement of the gardens and flowers. The 'sundries exhibitors' arrive on Monday morning, making Eastern Avenue a sea of lorries, vans and cars surrounded by discarded cardboard, paper and polystyrene packaging.

Until the mid 1970s, visitors could only enquire about or place orders for goods from these exhibitors, but now they can actually buy smaller items to take home from the Show — and do so with a vengeance.

Some of the trade exhibitors have, like the nurserymen, been coming to Chelsea for as long as anyone can remember. The Army and Navy Stores, of Victoria Street, for instance, with their books on one stand and floral printed garden furniture on another; Drew, Clark and Co of Leyton with their ladders, steps and trestles; E.H. Taylor, who have shown beehives and bee-keeping equipment since 1912.

Hatchards Bookshop, which played such a significant role in the founding of the Society, moves in with a good part of its gardening and natural history department, under the management of the appropriately named Sue Page. Household names like ICI are there, whose large stand in Main Avenue informs and advises visitors on how to protect their garden from pests and diseases, improve the quality of their lawn, roses or house plants and grow bigger and better vegetables.

Scaling the heights

Numerous mechanical aids to easier gardening will tempt those who fight a losing battle against the waywardness of nature. There are hedge trimmers and brush cutters, pruners, chain saws and log splitters; pneumatic sprayers, syringes, pumps and generators; small tractors, cultivators and rotovators — and, of course, lawnmowers. The gleaming, modern machines displayed by proud manufacturers on stands in Northern Avenue are a far cry from the horse drawn models of the early Shows. Now they hover or rotate, and work with the simplicity of a vacuum cleaner; they are driven by electricity or small petrol engines, and range from a tiny, lightweight gadget for those with a pocket handkerchief of grass to the throbbing sophistication of a 'ride-on' machine for the gardener with rolling acres.

On open stands on the opposite side of Northern Avenue, complete sheds, conservatories and summerhouses are erected — and greenhouses. These, too, have changed with the times. The timber-framed house, made individually to order, has largely been replaced by mass produced, aluminium-framed structures with all manner of automated 'extras' — self-opening vents, watering systems, capillary matting, insulation, frost predictors and simple electric or oil fired heaters to replace those boilers and pipes of the past.

As the manufacturers display their wares, work in the marquee reaches a climax that is quietly tense rather than frenzied. On the gardens, we try to have finished work by Monday morning. There are always last minute jobs, although

Decision time as the judges take a vote

these are often hindered by meetings with old friends and acquaintances who happen to pass, and conversations with members of the Press gathering material for their Show report. Whatever the interruptions, everything must be ready by four o'clock for the most nerve-racking moment of the Show — the judging of the gardens, the marquee exhibits of flowers and plants, and the floral arrangements. On Monday morning, Allan Sawyer will have assessed the nature of all the marquee exhibits, and categorised them as suitable for judging by a particular, specialist committee.

The committees are made up of enthusiasts and experts in their field — some of whom are, inevitably, exhibitors themselves, and others who are universally acknowledged for their depth of learning and experience. The gardens are judged not by a committee, but by the members of the RHS Council. Many of the judges used to arrive at the Show on Monday morning, and would see exhibits for the first time when judging, but Lord Aberconway has urged both committee and Council members to look around on Saturday and Sunday, and

And for the garden that has everything . . .

familiarise themselves with what exhibitors are trying to achieve, so that they can contribute to discussions. The President himself can be seen walking slowly around the Show every day from Friday onwards, talking to exhibitors and giving occasional advice on anything that he feels might detract from the judges' favour.

When the moment arrives, groups of gentlemen in suits, often with bowler hats, gather together, accompanied by the occasional lady, and commence their tours of inspection. As the scrutiny and muttered discussions take place, exhibitors are required to stand well out of earshot, able only to see the show of hands that may seal their fate. There is a long wait until Tuesday morning for the verdicts, for later in the evening the recommendations for medals made by the judging committees will be discussed by the full Council, and final decisions taken. The Council takes a broader view of standards right across the various types of exhibitors, and may sometimes nudge upwards or downwards the original recommendation for individual awards, if they feel an exhibit has been judged too harshly, or does not quite attain the quality of a similar award in a different category.

For the moment, all these considerations are temporarily cast aside by judges and exhibitors alike, and preparations begin for the Chelsea Show's most exciting climax — the Royal visit.

CHAPTER 5

WHILST THE judging committees make their tours of inspection, the grounds are cleared of all people except those with a special badge that must be conspicuously worn. Without it, you will be sent packing by at least one burly policeman — with it, you will qualify for the ultimate privilege that showing at Chelsea can bestow — an intimate glimpse of many of the leading members of the Royal Family.

Almost from the time it was founded, the RHS has been fortunate in the encouragement its work has received through the patronage of members of the Royal Family. Queen Charlotte became the first Royal patron in 1816, and her signature appears on an illuminated page in the Society's Obligation Book. This set a precedent, and the exquisitely embellished autographs of subsequent British and foreign patrons and Honorary Fellows are still in the possession of the Lindley Library. The most recent addition is the autograph of HM Queen Elizabeth II, who, together with HM Queen Elizabeth the Queen Mother is the Society's present Patron.

It was under the patronage of Queen Victoria in 1861 that the Society received a new charter, adding the title 'Royal' to its name, and in celebration of the sixtieth anniversary of that Queen's accession to the throne, in 1897, established the Victoria Medal of Honour in Horticulture. This medal — its highest award — is given to persons deserving of special honour, the recipients being limited to

The Queen and Prince Philip insist on seeing the Show despite the rain

sixty at any one time (the number was later increased to sixty-three, the number of years of Queen Victoria's reign). Present holders of the V.M.H. include the President, Lord Aberconway, and HM The Queen Mother.

By tradition, members of the Royal family are given a preview of the Chelsea Show. Nowadays, no official opening ceremony is performed; instead, this is an opportunity for the Royal guests to look at exhibits and talk to exhibitors in an informal way, before the Show is open to the public and members of the Society. The visit used to take place on the Tuesday morning of Chelsea week, with access for RHS members in the afternoon. Now, it occurs early on Monday evening, while the judges finish looking at the exhibits, and before they discuss and agree their final decisions on the awards that will be made.

At this time, the Show can be seen at its very best — every bloom at its peak of freshness; every leaf, every blade of grass in place; every path swept clean and every fountain or waterfall sweetly playing in a clear, leafless pool. It is a matter of pride that everything should be as near perfect as possible to withstand the Royal scrutiny.

Only authorised members of the Press and one representative of each exhibitor may remain in the grounds, along with a number of RHS staff, various officials and those responsible for the considerable security.

As the last unauthorised visitors are hastened on their way, the Show undergoes a speedy transformation. Litter is collected; workmen with large brooms sweep the avenues, and are closely followed by water carts spraying the ground — all as near as is practical to the unrolling of a red carpet. Exhibitors who only half-an-hour before were putting the final touches to their arrangements, clad in old working clothes and wellington boots, now reappear scrubbed and besuited, or sporting smart dresses and hats.

Gradually, a late afternoon peace settles, in place of the urgent bustle of the day. Emotions veer between relief that at last everything is completed and anxiety as to whether the final results will prove equal to the occasion. Very few people know the precise time that the cars will arrive, and the mounting tension and anticipation can be felt throughout the Show. Small groups of exhibitors stand and converse, but the conversations are only superficial, for everybody is watching, listening and waiting — and perhaps daring to hope that the fruits of their labours will receive a glance of Royal approval. Outside the gate, a small crowd of enthusiastic Royalists gathers on the pavement. Inside, the President and members of the Council wait to greet their guests. A bevy of photographers and cameramen are ready to spring into action; they will follow the principal guests everywhere, hoping to capture the perfect picture.

Suddenly, word goes around, 'They're here', and a small cheer is heard as the first limousine glides slowly through the gate and purrs to a halt. Its occupants are greeted by two footmen in splendid uniform, and the member of Council who will conduct that particular party (probably one of six or seven parties) of Royal visitors around the Show.

Although the preparations are thorough, not even the President can be certain exactly what will ensue, for this is a delightfully relaxed Royal event, where no detailed procedure is laid down. Each year, the Society invites all the Royal households to attend the preview of the Show, but the guest list is not finalised until a week or so before the event.

The guests arrive in reverse order of precedence, the last limousine usually bearing HM The Queen, often accompanied by the Duke of Edinburgh. Whenever possible, Queen Elizabeth the Queen Mother also attends. Her knowledge and fondness of gardening are well known; her captivating charm and deep interest in all she sees endear her to every exhibitor. The Royal family is said to treasure this appearance in such a cheerful, informal atmosphere, and, intriguingly, to welcome the opportunity of meeting en masse. A few years ago, some of the Royal visitors had not seen each other for the previous four or five weeks.

After being conducted around the Show, and talking to some of the exhibitors, the guests are entertained to a champagne tea in the President's tent, and it is taken as a great compliment to the Society that they don't usually start to leave until well after the appointed time. This informality makes the Royal tour of Chelsea a somewhat unpredictable affair, for the guests often have their own interests and preferences, to which deference must, of course, be made.

The late Princess Alice of Athlone was well known for her great enthusiasm

The Queen and Queen Mother have always appreciated the floral tributes they receive

for Chelsea, and even in quite recent memory caused her guides difficulty in keeping up with her pace. One Council member recalls the following incident, which occurred in the early 1970s:

'My wife and I conducted Princess Alice around the Show, and wherever we went, from exhibit to exhibit, her knowledge not only of horticulture but also of many stand holders, was amazing. Consequently, after touring the Show, she had collected quite a bouquet of flowers — specimens handed to her by various exhibitors. Eventually, we met up with other members of the Royal Family, and the Princess was asked by one, "Auntie, where did you get that loot?" "That is not loot," came the reply, "that is floral appreciation from my friends."'

A determination on the part of the Royal family to view the Show in their own way is by no means recent, and was, perhaps, even more marked in the past. King Edward VIII, who later became the Duke of Windsor, was a great horticulturist, with a particular knowledge of rhododendrons. As Prince of Wales, in the early 1930s, he would visit Chelsea with the official Royal party, and then return on public days, mingling with the crowds and viewing the exhibits in closer detail. A visitor who was a young woman at the time, remembers a small, unmistakable figure with straw-like hair; he was, of course, extremely popular, and would attract a small crowd of followers, although they always maintained a discreet distance.

In 1934, the Prince took a liking to a small rock garden exhibited at Chelsea, and ordered it to be transferred in its entirety to the garden at Fort Belvedere at the close of the Show. If the exhibitor was surprised at the commission, how much greater must have been his surprise when the Prince himself pitched in to help with the later dismantling of the garden!

The Prince of Wales shared his love of gardens with his mother, Queen Mary, and Royal visits to Chelsea were perhaps even less formal in the reign of King George V and Queen Mary than they are now. However, if informality was the order of the day for Royalty, the same was certainly not true of exhibitors, for bowler hat, black jacket and striped trousers were de rigeur for those gentlemen who would come under the Royal gaze, and in the apparently superior confines of the Orchid Tent, tails were always worn.

But if Queen Mary was an enthusiast, the reverse was true of her husband. Surely the most amusing and revealing tale of King George at Chelsea is told by the President's late mother, Lady Christabel Aberconway in her book *A Wiser Woman?* (Hutchinson, 1966):

'My husband, being President of the Royal Horticultural Society, had the privilege of taking the King and Queen round the Chelsea Flower Show. I was told that I would walk in front with the King, and that at all costs I must try to prevent him from marching forward too quickly, while my husband would follow with Queen Mary, whose progress, because of her intense interest in all she saw, was always slow. I foresaw that it wouldn't be an easy task.

'Ten minutes before King George and Queen Mary were due to arrive, a message came from Buckingham Palace: "The King is in a bad temper; please

King George and Queen Mary arrive

take him round the shortest way." Since then I have tried in vain to discover who sent that message, that message which drained my courage.

'King George and Queen Mary arrived and we set forth. The King and I exchanged a few dreary remarks about the weather. Then I spoke of the Royal Hospital at Chelsea and of Nell Gwynn. The King brightened; it was obvious that he was not interested in flowers, so I thought that ancestors and history were a possibility. We were getting on quite well, discussing, if I remember rightly, the Duke of Clarence and the butt of Malmsey wine, and were getting on to wine in general, when four or five photographers jumped out, knelt down, and photographed the King. He stopped dead. "This is intolerable, intolerable," he said. "They've taken quite enough photographs of me today; these journalists — these journalists — I'm going back to the Palace."

'I suppose I should have murmured about the disappointment of everyone present; instead I risked all, which some might call "a gaffe", by saying: "Sir, who has encouraged journalists more than yourself: have you not ennobled Northcliffe, Rothermere, Beaverbrook?"

'It was touch and go. I was given an "old-fashioned look", and then in a low voice he said: "Well, well, yes, yes, let's go on."

'I then showed him a sad little flower, telling him that the poor little thing was called "Lousewort". This amused him, and he called up equerries to ask them if they knew the name of the innocent little plant.

'Going through the big tent he pointed to some mauve and orange flowers placed close together: "horrid colours: pink and blue, pink and blue, those are the colours that should always go together." I then scored another mark: "Well, sir," I said, "I took my young daughter to the Zoo the other day, and tried to prevent her seeing certain portions of a monkey's anatomy; but she observed the creature and asked, in a carrying voice: 'Are those pink and blue patches *meant* to be the monkey's bottom?'"

'This delighted King George and after that, every year at Chelsea, he told me how much he had enjoyed the afternoon. His enjoyment became so noticeable that in 1931 the Press commented on it, the *Daily Express* saying: "The King, I should add, seemed in excellent form, and laughed heartily during almost his entire tour of the show, which he inspected under the eyes of the Honourable Mrs Henry McLaren." But, alas, he wasn't interested in flowers, though they often suggested to him unusual questions such as: "I wonder where all that moss came from?" I refrained from answering that it surely had come from the Royal Gardens in Windsor Great Park, but undoubtedly it had.'

Waiting with anticipation . . .

On occasion, an unpredictable incident may occur that is due entirely to a 'gaffe' on the part of an exhibitor, and a few years ago this happened to us.

We were showing a small garden in conjunction with *Practical Householder* magazine, so the design included a number of garden projects for the keen do-it-yourselfer. Among them was a table/workbench that could be folded flat against a timber screen, revealing only a set of shelves for storage. When open, the shelves provided support for the table top and stood rigid, but as the table was lifted, they swung free.

This innovation had been noted with some fascination by the judging committee, and was pointed out by Mr Louis Russell to a senior member of the Royal Family, whom he was conducting around the Show. As we hastened to comply with the suggestion that the folding table might be demonstrated, the lady stepped forward with interest to see more closely. Some garden sundries had been positioned on the shelves by a willing helper, anxious to perfect the finishing touches; unbeknown to us, among these was a large glass bottle of liquid tomato fertilizer.

As we enthusiastically lifted the table, the shelves swung free, and in a split second the bottle had fallen and smashed on the paving, splashing its thin, brown contents on the legs and skirt of both the Royal person and her lady-in-waiting.

There was panic, confusion and sheer, frozen terror. The gentlemen hastily proffered handkerchieves and reassurances, and the lady-in-waiting anxiously asked whether the bottle contained any substance that might be harmful to the skin, but the Royal lady herself remained charming and unruffled, although obviously concerned and certainly surprised. We could hear ourselves apologising repeatedly and helplessly, but the event was graciously dismissed. Later, we were overwhelmed with relief, gratitude and admiration when we heard that a letter of thanks for an enjoyable visit had been sent to the Secretary the very next day, but it was some time before we could bring ourselves to repeat the story.

When the nation is celebrating a specific Royal event, Chelsea exhibitors can be relied upon to respond by making a special effort, with some imaginative results. Appropriately, this is particularly true of the Royal Parks.

And suspense rewarded

The Royal Parks include gardens at historic Royal establishments such as Hampton Court, Greenwich and Osborne House on the Isle of Wight, but the Chelsea exhibits are undertaken by London establishments — Regent's Park and the Central Royal Parks Group, which includes St James's, Hyde Park and the gardens of Kensington Palace and Buckingham Palace.

Superintendent of the Central Royal Parks is Bob Legge, and both he and his predecessor, Ashley Stevenson — now Bailiff of the Royal Parks — have become closely identified with the Chelsea exhibits. A distinctive style manifests itself in stunning, informal arrangements, such as lock gates, a water wheel or a woodland garden teeming with flowers and plants that give the impression of almost overgrown maturity. But Bob Legge is also capable of impressive formality, such as the Royal Parks' Chelsea tribute to the marriage of Prince Charles and Lady Diana Spencer, in the form of the Prince of Wales' feathers reproduced in carpet bedding, using the tiny, muted green and red foliage of Helxine, rather than garish flowers, and backed by grass and gravel.

This first official contribution to the wedding celebrations met with the Queen's approval on her visit to the Show, and was later transferred to Hyde Park, in a position opposite the Hilton Hotel, where it was admired throughout the summer. This was a particularly busy summer for the Group, which was also responsible for some of London's wedding decorations, including hanging baskets in The Mall, and gold and white flowers in the beds around the flagstaffs at

The Queen and Princess Margaret tour the Show in 1981

Buckingham Palace. All the plants used, both here and at Chelsea, were, as usual, grown by the Central Parks staff at their glasshouses in Hyde Park and Regent's Park, or at the nursery for hardy stock at Roehampton, near Richmond Park.

The Queen Mother's eightieth birthday was marked by a rather different exhibit, staged by the National Farmers Union. As regular exhibitors at Chelsea, their displays of mountains and rows of perfect, polished fruit and vegetables are a familiar sight to visitors. Less expected was the 'Queen Mother's Crown', an intriguing headpiece made from such unlikely material as white cauliflower curds, and topped by strawberry 'rubies' and a Bramley apple.

The most universal tribute at Chelsea in recent years was in celebration of the Queen's Silver Jubilee, when many exhibitors included plants with Royal connections or silver foliage on their stands. The Royal Parks made an even more spectacular crown (on the Monument site, as might be expected), which stood twenty feet high, used 11,000 individual plants — predominantly silver against a 'purple velvet' background of African violets — and was acknowledged by Her Majesty as a truly magnificent effort.

Roses have become an almost traditional tribute to Royal Persons, and this occasion was no exception, with the first public showing of the elegant 'Silver Jubilee' rose bred by Alex Cocker. The sweetly perfumed, large pink blooms are complemented by glossy, deep green leaves on long, sturdy stems; hardly surprising that it has proved a popular plant for these qualities, as well as for its emotional and patriotic significance. 'Royal Salute' is a neat, bushy miniature rose with prolific deep pink flowers, and was bred by Sam McGredy in New Zealand. It, too, was launched for the Silver Jubilee at Chelsea — this time by John Mattock and Sons, who gave it a rousing fanfare from a regimental trumpeter in full dress regalia.

Princess Alexandra in the 1960s — as always, taking a keen interest

Such tributes are more difficult to make tastefully in a garden, but we wanted to offer our own contribution to the celebrations, and eventually decided to include in the planting several plants of the rhododendron 'Elizabeth'. As a specimen of dwarf habit, with masses of vibrant scarlet flowers, this is a splendid plant for any small garden, and therefore worth including in its own right. Although we did not know how the name of 'Elizabeth' was given, we felt that its significance to the event would anyway be appreciated. The dozen or so plants were grown to perfection for us by Notcutts Nurseries and, having positioned them in the garden close to some silver foliage, we were quite pleased with our efforts.

Later, on his usual tour of the Show, giving advice and hints to exhibitors, the President stopped and noticed rhododendron 'Elizabeth', commenting on its usefulness as a garden plant. As we told him that its presence was in honour of Her Majesty's Silver Jubilee, he looked at us with almost pitying amusement, and explained with great delight and a twinkle in his eye that rhododendron 'Elizabeth' was named after his sister. 'If there is time,' he added, 'I will tell the Queen that you have planted in her honour a rhododendron named after my sister; she'll be amused I'm sure.'

In the event, the Royal visit was shorter than usual, due to the large number of engagements in that busy year, and Her Majesty did not visit our garden. Perhaps it was just as well. But the President's sister did see it, and, knowing nothing of what had gone before, remarked to us as she passed, 'Oh, that's rhododendron "Elizabeth". It's named after me, you know.' We knew.

For exhibitors, the Royal visit is an exciting, exhilarating climax to months of planning and days or weeks of work at Chelsea. When the distinguished guests have departed, and dusk starts to fall, there is a feeling of great tiredness and slight deflation. Whatever fate is in store from the judges, whatever success the actual Show may bring, the sense of comradeship experienced when everyone is working to a common end is over for another year. From tomorrow morning, we are all there as individual exhibitors and must, to some extent, vie to interest visitors in our goods or services — must answer their questions and queries with patience and politeness, trying to ignore our aching feet and to conceal our hands, still stained and roughened from several days of handling plants, peat and stone.

We walk slowly back to the car, entering the now silent, empty marquee by one of its few unfastened flaps. It is like venturing into a vast, secret, forbidden garden, where everything is unnaturally still, and our footsteps make no sound. In the heavy yellow light, the heady perfumes of a thousand different blooms mingle with the earthy smell of damp, warm grass. Soft, single petals of pure white, velvet pinks and blues, hot reds and yellows combine to form a bold, yet somehow blurred kaleidoscope of colour with, here and there, a relief of quiet green. On and on, further than the eye can see, the flowers hug the ground, scale the wooden tent poles and peer and nod over porcelain vases and rough hessian. They are everywhere, seeming to hold their soft breath in hushed anticipation of the admiring crowds that tomorrow will bring.

CHAPTER 6

HE GATES of the great and famous Chelsea Show are opened at eight o'clock sharp on Tuesday morning. Now, after all the sweat and tears, the Royal Horticultural Society and its exhibitors prepare to share their annual triumph of achievement with an eager public. But even before this early hour anxious exhibitors must grit their teeth and discover the verdict of the judging committees and the Council on their own individual achievement. On Monday night when the final list of awards and medals has been drafted, the Shows office staff has the lengthy task of writing out handsome embossed certificate cards, each bearing an impression of the medal it represents. When the writing is completed, the certificates are delivered to the stands. The distribution is an informal affair quite without ceremony, pomp or circumstance. In the case of the gardens, Allan Sawyer rides his trusty bike along Main Avenue and merely tosses each certificate on to the exhibit in the manner of an American newspaper boy. We try to arrive as early as possible and approach our garden with trepidation. It seems a very long walk from the gate, and we hope that no fellow exhibitor will break the news to us before we have had a chance to see for ourselves.

When that small card is eventually in exhibitors' shaking hands, most of them react in one of three ways. If the award is lower than they felt their exhibit warranted, for its own merits and in comparison with others, there may be bitter disappointment. Where did they go wrong? Did the judges really appreciate what they were trying to do? Worse is the knowledge that they must wait another year before the chance to try again.

If they know this year's stand was not up to Gold Medal standard but receive an award in line with their own expectations, then there is either some pleasure and satisfaction or, at worst, a quiet resignation.

The third possibility for which they had hardly dared hope is that they should actually be awarded the Royal Horticultural Society's Gold Medal. Those long-standing exhibitors who have received a Gold every year for as long as they can remember are justifiably proud of having once again attained their own high standard. But even they can never quite experience that elation, that sense of pride and tremendous achievement that is only felt when a Gold Medal comes after years of effort — when it represents the pinnacle of success after a slow graduation through all the lower awards. After that experience, the Show seems a different place and you are swept along through the week on a tide of congratulations and good wishes from friends who share your joy.

The medal itself is not received until some months later. The Gold Medal is little bigger than a ten pence piece and comes in a small box inscribed 'John Pinches London'. It is well worth waiting for and a sobering reminder of the great traditions not only of more than sixty Chelsea Shows but also of Wedgwood, Banks and all those pioneering spirits who founded the Society and kept it alive. One is very proud to feel a small sense of belonging to those traditions.

Disappointment, resignation or elation are soon jolted back to more immediate practicalities when the gates are opened. Tuesday is Members' Day, when the Show is open only to RHS members or junior members who already hold a card or who have joined at the gate. It is officially known as the members' 'Private View', inferring a rather small, exclusive preview, but this day is now always so busy that the view is anything but private. Nevertheless there is an air of exclusivity and exhibitors must certainly be on their toes, for this is indeed a well-informed public made up of highly-dedicated gardeners and plant lovers, both amateur and professional.

Although the social distinctions that were so much a part of Chelsea in the past have now largely disappeared, a sense of occasion remains on this day in particular. The keen-eyed can spot many well-known faces in the crowd — some of them regulars. There are politicians, actors, television personalities; all are united by a love of gardening, and most are much more interested in seeing than being seen.

The event through which Chelsea retains its importance in the Social Calendar is the 'President's Tea Party' which takes place on Tuesday afternoon in the President's Tea Tent. The guests are eminent gardeners and people closely associated with the RHS as well as diplomats, overseas visitors and prominent public figures, and the occasion warrants reports in *Vogue*, *The Tatler* and the essential 'Jennifer's Diary' of *Harpers & Queen*. The very existence of this genteel echo of the past is a fact of which most visitors to Chelsea are quite unaware.

The pilgrimage to see the results of man's handiwork in the miraculous natural world of plants hardly ceases for four days. The Show is open to RHS members from 8 am to 8 pm on Tuesday; to the public it is open for the same hours on Wednesday and Thursday and from 8 am to 5 pm on Friday. The admission charge decreases as the week goes on, and in an attempt to spread crowds throughout the day the RHS now makes a reduced charge for entry after 3.30 pm on Wednesday and Thursday. For safety reasons, children under five are not admitted. Dogs, too, are forbidden but escorts are on hand for blind people and facilities are available for disabled people in wheelchairs, who are admitted at any time.

There are two main entrances to the Show — one from Royal Hospital Road and the other from the Chelsea Embankment. Taxis, buses and Underground trains from Victoria are full to overflowing with visitors making their way to the Northern 'Hospital' entrance and a second exit is in operation at Sloane Square Underground station to get people on their way as quickly and smoothly as possible. Once out of the station, there is no need to ask directions — just fall in with the eagerly anticipatory crocodile and join the brisk, purposeful walk to Lower Sloane Street and around the corner.

Of the crowd you join, some ladies may be wearing the traditional flamboyant hat with a smart suit or dress, but these days your companions are more likely to be wearing sensible flat walking shoes with comfortable clothes.

Visitors who arrive by car are able to leave their vehicle in Battersea Park, where every available area is opened up for the purpose. The later you arrive, the longer will be your walk to the entrance of the Park, but you will not have to face what often used to be a blustery walk over Chelsea Bridge, because the Society now runs a mini bus service to ferry visitors from the Park to the Show's Bull Ring entrance. The service is most welcome, for visitors need all their energy to walk around the Show itself!

From whichever direction they come, many of the crowds will take the sensible precaution of bringing macintosh or umbrella and some will also come equipped with sandwiches and thermos flask. Exhibitors never cease to be amazed at the persistence and dedication of visitors in pursuit of one aim — finding a likely spot for a picnic.

To build a low wall at the edge of a garden or stand is fatal, for in no time it will invite a flock of cheerful visitors, perched side by side and quietly munching sandwiches. A flurry of indignation greets the polite request to move, although chairs are available in the Show and in Ranelagh Gardens and there is a Shelter Tent in case of rain. Recently one persistent 'squatter' positioned himself on the low stone step at the front of a manufacturer's stand and fell blissfully asleep for an hour or so.

After the customary bag search by security staff, visitors pay at one of a series of turnstile entrances at the gates. Responsibility for the organisation of the entrances lies with RHS Assistant Secretary, Geoffrey Harvey, who has found that the most satisfactory arrangement for staffing the turnstiles is to recruit the lads of his local football club! Just as well if they are in good athletic training, for they can be assured of a busy week, collecting money at such a rate that there is barely time to count it before depositing it safely in the bank.

Anyone who has ever joined the queue for Chelsea will not need to be told that

Taking a break . . .

this is an extremely popular show, attracting up to 70,000 visitors in one day. On occasions the queue for the Bull Ring entrance has stretched right along the Embankment and some considerable distance down Chelsea Bridge Road and the wide approach roadway from Royal Hospital Road to the Show gates becomes a solid mass of people.

The Show is extremely crowded at times, particularly in the middle of the day, and another of Geoffrey Harvey's tasks is to monitor the number of visitors entering the grounds against those leaving through a series of checkers. He must use these figures to decide when there is a danger of the crowds becoming totally unmanageable and in that event the gates would be closed — a situation that has occurred only very rarely. Encouraged by the RHS the wise visit the Show either early in the day or much later.

The role of the police in helping to manage both crowds and traffic is a vital and valuable one. The majority of the men and women responsible are based at Chelsea Police Station, although additional personnel are drafted in from the Metropolitan area, and 'Special' policemen also play a part. Some weeks before the Show warning signs to traffic are posted in the area, and during Chelsea week every effort is made to keep the increased traffic flowing smoothly — efforts that are usually successful.

The major role of the police inside the Show is one of security, particularly during the Royal visit, but inevitably the temporary police post, close to the Embankment entrance, deals with a range of visitors' problems and enquiries and if specialist help is needed, the post is in communication with Chelsea Police Station by radio and telephone.

Once inside the grounds, the first task of visitors is to orientate themselves and discover where to find everything. Plans of the grounds and marquees and lists of exhibitors are all contained in the Show Catalogue, but if they are still in doubt, visitors can seek advice from the RHS enquiry office near the top of Main Avenue. This is staffed by the Society's own employees, and a tour of duty at the desk requires extreme patience and resilience. There are the regular questions to which one would have thought the answers were obvious ('Where is the marquee?' and 'Where are the flowers?' are two evergreens) and then there are forceful complaints — perhaps about those perennial bones of contention, the catering and the ladies' toilets — and the occasional visitor who insists on a refund of his entrance fee because it has rained.

Exhibitors too find it remarkable that each year a distinct pattern of questions develops quite quickly. As the visitors file past, and one by one ask the same question or make the same comment as if performing a well-rehearsed routine, we cannot suppress a faint smile of amusement.

In fact, visitors are in the main good humoured and often ready for a joke. A few pass disparaging comments, but those who admire and appreciate the work that has gone into exhibitors' stands make the whole enterprise worthwhile. As Allan Sawyer says, gardeners are nice people and very few exhibitors remain unmoved by the overwhelming kindness and generosity they receive from so many of their public at Chelsea.

That same public is equally capable of asking questions that are somewhat

Even bad weather doesn't seem to affect the good humour of the crowd unusual. There was the lady who wanted advice from Fisons on the lowest growing bush variety of tomato, so that the plants could grow on the roof of the canal boat in which she lived, and still be able to pass comfortably under bridges.

John Mattock remembers well the occasion when his firm celebrated its centenary with an exhibit on the Monument Stand, and took the unusual step of surrounding the Chillianwallah Monument itself with water, leaving it much more exposed to view than previous exhibitors had done. On the first day he was approached by an old customer who sidled up to him and asked, 'Look Mr Mattock, I know it's your firm's centenary, but are you really going to take that great big monument with all your employees' names on to every show in the country this year?'

It is sometimes said by visitors that the Chelsea Show 'looks the same every year.' They see little discernable difference from Show to Show, but the organisers and most exhibitors would take a different view. As John Cowell points out, some ten per cent of exhibitors change from year to year, and of those that remain as regulars nearly all try to present themselves in a different way each time. Certainly the gardens are completely different, for there would be little point in going to all that trouble to make a near replica of a previous exhibit.

There is something indefinable about Chelsea — something that can only be called the Show's character — that is always discernibly different to those who know it well. Perhaps it is only by looking back that we can appreciate to what extent the Chelsea Show has reflected social change — and in doing so must, of necessity, have changed its own character, although remaining essentially the same in spirit. This is true not only of the distant past, but even in recent years. In the last period of economic restraint — the 'freeze' of the mid 1970s — there was tremendous enthusiasm for vegetable-growing and self sufficiency, and Chelsea exhibits reflected this. Yet in 1981, a year of dire economic depression, there seemed to be a new spirit — of escapism perhaps? — reflected in an emphasis on decoration and ornamentation rather than practical gardening.

Nevertheless, in spite of recessions and depressions, gardening still booms and continues to be one of this nation's most popular pastimes, and the gardeners continue to come to Chelsea in their thousands — to look, to learn, to buy or place their orders, and simply to have a good day out. They come not only from London and the Home Counties; Thursday and Friday are, by tradition, days when coach trips to Chelsea are organised from nearly all parts of the British Isles. They come from Scotland, Wales, Yorkshire, East Anglia, the Midlands and the West Country — gardening clubs, Women's Institutes, allotment societies and small groups of friends or relatives.

More and more visitors come, too, from abroad, particularly the United States. Overseas visitors are often fervently interested, and one Australian lady asked if she could have a pebble from our garden to go with the collection of stones from different parts of England that she was taking back home!

Seasoned showgoers have their favourite plants and exhibits that they would not miss for the world. Those who have done their homework insist on seeing stands described in Press previews of the Show, but first time visitors with little knowledge of specific plants and exhibits are usually overwhelmed and often quite incredulous, for the reaction to displays of plants from all seasons in endless variety, in fulsome bloom or luscious with fruit, is quite simply one of speechless disbelief.

Although the character of the Show may change from year to year, among the exhibits that visitors see will be many hardy perennials, but they will also see some that have captured the popular imagination only in the last few years, and others that are intriguing one-offs — a special effort made for that Show alone, never to be seen again.

Of course, some of the Show's facilities never change — in particular the band, which is as essential to Chelsea as the marquee and the Hospital's pensioners; the existence of a band is a tradition that dates back to those very early flower shows at Chiswick, Kensington and the Temple Gardens. By permission of the Lieutenant-Colonel commanding the Regiment, the band of the Grenadier Guards plays at every Chelsea Show. The reputation of a military band is subject to peaks and troughs over the years, but the Royal Horticultural

Visitors enjoy music from the bandstand

Society has not wavered in its loyalty to the Grenadiers — a loyalty apparently endorsed by the crowds who regularly gather around the Bandstand in Ranelagh Gardens on each afternoon, in rain or shine, but particularly in shine.

The scene is gentle, timeless and essentially British. Taking a break from the serious business of studying the plants and gardens, visitors sit on chairs or lounge on the grass, picnic or queue for ice creams. Following the programme of music printed in the Show Catalogue they listen quietly and intently, eyes half closed perhaps, and applaud politely at the end of each piece — applause acknowledged equally politely by Director of Music Major D.R. Kimberley on behalf of the band. Each day his musicians will play some twenty-eight separate pieces of music in two sessions — 2.30 to 4.30 pm and 5 to 7 pm — pieces by composers as varied as Tchaikovsky and John Lennon, Berlioz and Bernstein.

More practical facilities in addition to the catering marquees, two St John Ambulance Posts and public telephones are the bank and post office. Each year the Victoria Street branch of the National Westminster Bank sets up a temporary office in a portable building with cheerful blue and white striped awning at the Embankment end of Main Avenue, and 'cordially invites' visitors and exhibitors alike to make use of its services. The service cannot be considered anything but efficient, for we carelessly left a bank book in there on the last afternoon of the Show, only for it to be returned via our own bank a few days' later with a brief and somehow poignant note, 'Left on the counter at the Chelsea Flower Show. Returned with Compliments.'

But the exhibits are what the crowds have really come to see, and they are rarely disappointed. Enter the Show from the Chelsea Embankment and the vast marquee, with all its promise, is ahead of you. But resist that temptation for a while, and wander along Southern Road and among stands — either built in against the side of the marquee or out in the open on the grass — where there is furniture of all kinds to make your garden leisure a little more stylish, comfortable and luxurious.

By courtesy of the Army and Navy Stores you can take a cushioned seat at a vast French table set for a lazy summertime lunch for ten. Even the plates and napkins match the green or red striped fabric of the parasols that gently shade you from the pitching sun, and when lunch is over, imagine yourself simply sliding on to a cushioned, slatted sun-lounger with drinks trolley to hand.

For those with simpler tastes there are rustic timber picnic tables or traditional Victorian styles in wrought aluminium, and the unashamedly idle can choose from a wealth of floral-patterned swinging hammocks with fringed canopy and deep, soft cushions.

If you doubt the reliability of the British summer, then there is no shortage of choice of summerhouses, with or without weather vane on the roof and curtains at the window. Knights of Reigate have for many years been purveyors of high quality, solid wooden garden buildings, their interiors cool, shaded and smelling pungently of cedar.

Something more unusual is offered by Machin Designs, a much younger firm whose conservatories and pavilions are reminiscent of Edwardian elegance and even Eastern minarets, their curved roofs often topped by a graceful spire.

Here, too, there are exhibitors of pots, statues and garden ornaments, one of whom once took the trouble to have a tiny authentic Japanese garden made in which to display their reproductions of Oriental figures and a snow lantern. There are even wood burning stoves and a wrought iron spiral staircase for lovers of the traditional.

Awakened from your reverie of luxurious leisure, turn back towards the River and past banks of rhododendrons and azaleas in brilliant, 'fruit salad' shades of pink, red, orange and yellow, until you reach the Rock Garden Bank. Sadly, there have been few of the beloved, traditional style rock gardens in recent years. Their construction requires massive organisation of transport and machinery — skilled labour no longer being the freely available commodity that it was in the heyday of the rock garden — and to gain the necessary impact thousands of plants must be used, even in the simpler landscaping more suited to modern tastes and pockets.

Until 1981, the most notable recent example of its kind was a garden shown by a Mr Douglas Knight of Formby, Lancashire, who is well known for his exhibits at the Southport Show and made a layout using skilfully positioned slabs of light grey Westmorland slate, which has a dramatically flat, 'chiselled' face — the perfect setting for a cool, dancing mountain stream. Then Paul Temple, already well known in landscaping circles, scored a triumphant success with a rock garden in rugged, craggy Westmorland stone, hand picked from the

Choosing an ornament

A statue forms the focal point of a garden in Main Avenue by Peter Rogers

moors and dappled with moss. Both the Society and the public were delighted to see once again the stuff that garden lovers' dreams are made of.

In Main Avenue and on the Rock Bank there are altogether between ten and fourteen gardens each year, of all different types, sizes and characters. Some are pure fantasy for the average garden owner, who nevertheless likes to look, often lost to the world for a few moments in an oblivion of admiration and longing for such beauty, such perfection. Others are more practical and realistic — the sort of layout that is actually attainable with some hard work and a little investment, but every garden has at least one idea that can be adapted or imitated. The aim of most exhibitors is to stimulate the imagination of visitors, to encourage them to think of new possibilities.

Of the regular garden exhibitors, the *Daily Express* is the longest standing. The newspaper used to run a competition for garden design, construct the two best layouts at the Show and invite the public to vote a winner. This they always did with immense enthusiasm, and although the scheme ceased in the mid 1970s visitors still ask for the *'Express* competition'. Now, each garden is designed for the newspaper as a 'one-off' by Guy Farthing, son of *Daily Express* gardening correspondent Donald Farthing, who is a familiar figure at the Show, and the gardens are constructed by the landscape department of John Waterer Sons and Crisp, with plants that are still grown at the firm's Bagshot nursery.

Merrist Wood College of Agriculture is becoming equally familiar as a garden exhibitor. Each year, students from the landscape course design and build a garden, usually based on a distinct theme. One of the most interesting was on a conservation theme, using only natural materials — rustic timber for a gazebo and log rounds as steps and paths — with plants all indigenous to the British Isles, including a lawn of clover instead of grass.

There are still some individual designers to be found among the exhibitors. John Brookes was until recently a 'regular' whose gardens were sought out by visitors. His clean, modern designs with their concept of an 'outdoor room' have had a tremendous influence on contemporary landscape styles, and his formidable partnership with the *Financial Times* in the early 1970s resulted in some truly memorable Chelsea gardens.

Alternatively, designers may be associated with magazine sponsors — notably David Stevens who creates interest-filled small gardens for *Homes and Gardens*. Of the specialist gardening magazines, *Amateur Gardening* has combined with its experts Arthur Billitt and Percy Thrower — so familiar and popular among viewers of BBC television for more than two decades — to present model vegetable plots. *Popular Gardening* has shown gardens designed by Peter Rogers under the guidance of the magazine's longstanding editor, Fred Whitsey. Mr Whitsey is well known not only for this role but also for his position as gardening correspondent for the *Daily Telegraph*, where his Show report is essential reference for many a Tuesday visitor.

The media has come increasingly to appreciate the potential of Chelsea as an opportunity for low key promotion at a prestigious event. In 1976 we introduced London's Capital Radio to the Show, exhibiting a small town garden and taking part in the first ever live radio broadcast to be transmitted from Chelsea. Capital

Graham Rose, of the Sunday Times *and Dzaier Neil in the 'Wheelchair Garden'*

continues to exhibit with the station's current personality gardener, Cyril Fletcher.

The *Sunday Times*, too, is rapidly becoming a Chelsea regular, constructing at the Show the winning garden in its annual design competition. Even during the paper's long absence from the newsstands due to industrial dispute, gardening correspondent Graham Rose still 'showed the flag' at Chelsea with a small, modest town garden.

In 1981 the paper marked the International Year of Disabled People with a 'Wheelchair Garden' designed by a young man who well understands the problems, as his own wife is confined to a wheelchair. With raised beds for growing vegetables and flowers, a pond made from a bath tub and a conservatory and greenhouse for winter activities, the garden gave many ideas that could be adapted for people with various types and degrees of disability.

Another 'one-off' garden of a very different type seen by visitors to the 1980 show was a Dorset cottage garden made by the members of the Gardens and Allotments Society of the village of Beaminster in Dorset for the BBC programme 'The Big Time'.

The makers of the programme, which gives amateur enthusiasts the chance to live out their interests at top professional level, felt that the Chelsea Show would make an excellent subject matter. So, with the assistance of the Chairman of the Shows Committee, John Mattock, who had to be assured that the group of gardeners chosen would come up to standard, and with contributions of plants and materials from a number of seasoned trade exhibitors as well as from their own gardens, the villagers duly arrived to form what must surely have been one of the largest groups of people ever to plan and build a Chelsea garden, for this was truly a community effort.

Their activities were accompanied by television cameras much of the time, and their hard work duly rewarded by the receipt of the Society's Gold Medal for an idyllic cottage garden that captured the imagination of town and city dwellers in particular. As two of the consultants to the programme, we realised from the beginning how tremendously determined these amateurs were, and when it was all over they had discovered at first hand the draining and exhausting effect of the 'Big Time' at the world's greatest flower show.

Having had your fill of the patios, lawns, gazebos, pools and water features, the plant beds and vegetable plots, and feeling either fired with enthusiasm or depressed by the inadequacy of your own plot in comparison, make your way to an entrance to the great marquee. The President's one-way system is clearly — not to say ostentatiously — signed, and the crowds have become accustomed to the procedure. No longer do they queue at the first entrance they see, thinking that all others must be exits!

The stands are so varied, the colours so dazzling and the warm, perfumed air so sweetly pungent that for a moment you are lost for which way to turn, like a child overwhelmed by a wealth of Christmas toys, like Alice in a floral Wonderland. It all seems magical, unreal, simply unbelievable.

Here, too, the exhibits are a mixture of the familiar faces — both plants and people — and the unique appeal of newcomers or one-offs.

Among the favourites are Blackmore and Langdon, their stand a mass of brilliant colour. On either side tower six and seven foot delphiniums of intense azure and sapphire or soft powder blue, and in the middle are huge blousy, double begonia flowers in lemon, vermilion, scarlet and crimson — loud, vibrant colours that seem to shout for attention.

Equally larger than life are the clematis shown by Fisks. The single flowers as round as tea plates seem almost too much for their slender, winding stems, and yet they are light and delicate as muslin, their colours ranging from palest pink to lilac, indigo and deepest purple.

Roses are everywhere — the new varieties as firm cut flowers on straight, sturdy stems arranged in vases, and some of the older shrub roses as plants, with arching stems and soft, open blooms like damask. Their scent is engulfing and for a moment your senses swim, drowning in its heady waves.

Orchids may not now be regarded as the aristocrats of the plant world they once were, but still they are there in quiet, dignified splendour. Their form is timeless and mysterious as their names — *Odontoglossum, Odontonia* and *Vuylstekeara* — their curved, petals like snakes' heads, mottled brown, olive and blood red. The colours start to fade almost indiscernibly as the days go by, and for this reason, when an orchid is in the running for an Award of Merit, an experienced botanical artist is on hand on the Monday of Chelsea week. If the award is received, the flower will be painted there and then, its characteristics immediately and accurately recorded.

In contrast is the simple, bright cheerfulness of Michael Jefferson-Brown's daffodils, their sweet, fresh perfume reminiscent of the recent spring. They are not the only bulb flowers, for other exhibitors have black-eyed red and yellow tulips and gracefully unfurling flags of iris in ivory, ochre and blue.

Amid the resplendence of dazzling colour are quiet havens of green. One will

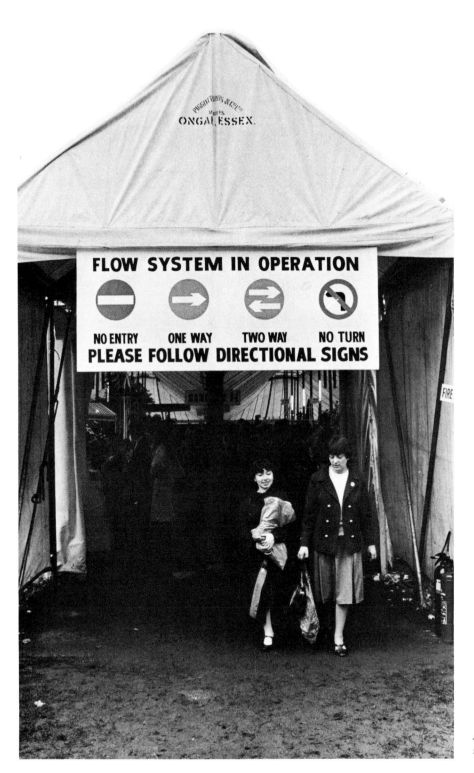

An unmistakable one-way system

almost certainly be a stunning array of conifers that bears the unmistakable mark of Bressingham Gardens. The still, small trees are perfect in form and although the overall impression is of green, there will also be the sharp, metallic blue of pines and cedars and the sulphurous yellow of *Chamaecyparis*. As a result of the work of Alan Bloom and his son Adrian, Bressingham is now renowned for its conifers, perennials and herbaceous plants in particular, and for its bold, pioneering work in plant publicity and marketing. Perhaps the best known of their new introductions was *Potentilla fruticosa* 'Red Ace', remarkable for the intense vermilion-red colour of its small, prolific, single flowers.

On its first showing in 1975 'Red Ace' was awarded the RHS First Class Certificate, but was also the object of some unwanted attention. Its unauthorised propagation for sale by anyone other than Blooms is prohibited, as the plant is protected by Plant Variety Rights, but an attempt was made to steal one of the plants from the display at the Society's Westminster Show in the New Hall. Consequently, on the occasion of 'Red Ace's Chelsea launch, the stand on which

Orchids in the marquee 1981

the innocent plants were displayed was watched over day and night by a uniformed security guard.

Other conifers, of a distinctly different character from those associated with Bressingham, will be shown by the exhibitors of plants grown in the Japanese Bonsai tradition, along with acers, flowering cherries, wisterias and many more. These miniaturised, often gnarled and twisted trees are fascinating, and have become very popular in recent years. But, as Mr Bromage of specialist growers Bromage and Young explains, there are many common misconceptions about Bonsai. Although hardy trees, most Chelsea visitors expect the plants to grow indoors and some even wonder whether they need water. There are, too, many fantastic claims about their age, but even Mr Bromage's estimate of 170 years as the maximum age of any Bonsai tree at present in this country is enough to give pause for thought.

Miniature trees were in fact bred in China even before the Japanese started the ancient custom of Bonsai, and these plants are known as Penjing. A recent

Fisons tomato plants laden with ripe fruit

Chelsea Show saw the first ever authentic Chinese exhibit, staged by the China National Native Produce and Animal By-Products Import and Export Corporation, and consisting of extraordinary, captivating, tiny scenarios of Penjing trees in a scaled-down landscape of rock and water. Each was individually illuminated on its own dais or alcove.

Great success has been enjoyed in just the last few years by Tony Clements' Nurseries, who show up to fifty different varieties of African violets — miniatures, trailers, variegateds, bi-colours — most of which have been hybridised in the United States. Tony Clements is convinced that the popularity of these discreet little plants with their dark, velvety leaves is due to the fact that they are small, not expensive to buy and flower all the year round.

Whilst African violets are easily recognisable, the small stand of Marston Exotics, exhibiting for the first time in 1981, comes as something of a shock to visitors, for under the eccentrically enthusiastic guidance of its founder, Adrian Slack, this company specialises in carnivorous plants. The stand is like a lunar landscape peopled by weird, long-legged or bog-creeping creatures coloured olive, lime, sepia and rust.

Inspired by a book he owned as a boy, Adrian Slack has had a lifelong interest in carnivorous plants and his work, together with that of amateur enthusiasts in the Carnivorous Plant Society, has brought to the attention of the public such delights as the trumpet pitchers (*Sarracenia*) which are highly efficient and decorative traps for houseflies and wasps. The 'Yellow Trumpet', for instance, is tall and erect with slender trumpet leaves crowned by a hood netted in crimson, and bears blooms of brimstone yellow in spring.

The marquee exhibitors are by no means exclusively professional growers and nurseries, for amateur devotees are still encouraged to show if they have something really special to offer.

Richard Cawthorne of South London is a landscape gardener by profession, but for some twenty-five years he has been making a collection of named violas and violettas with the object of saving them from extinction, as well as breeding new cultivars of his own. At Chelsea he shows up to 200 varieties of these shy, dainty flowers including such rarities as the old 'Show Pansies' of 1870 vintage and 'Viola Blue Cloud', which was popular in the 1890s and believed to be extinct until found growing in 1979.

An amateur of the old school is Mr Maurice L. Mason, who has built up a marvellous garden in the country at Fincham in Norfolk. On his annual expeditions to various parts of the world, Mr Mason collected a vast selection of what used to be known as stove plants, which he grows at Fincham under glass. In 1980 he dipped into this collection to stage, with his head gardener, a unique exhibit on the famous Monument Site. As one walked through the exhibit, the scene changed from jungle to savannah to Texas desert with cacti, bromeliads and exotic succulent plants — a poignant echo of a past that has all but disappeared.

As well as amateurs, there is a magnificent tradition of Chelsea exhibits by local authority parks departments and other public bodies. The London Borough of Newham recently staged an inspired dockland scene, with cranes loading

Visitors absorbed by an exhibit of exotic cacti and succulent plants

baskets of flowers on to similarly flower laden barges. Birmingham, Brighton, Liverpool, Hammersmith and even Telford Development Corporation have all made important contributions to Chelsea.

Slough Borough Council Parks Department has specialised in chrysanthemums and annuals over the years — carpets of huge specimens of antirrhinums, schizanthus or stocks, all positively bursting with health and vigour. One man who did a great deal to establish Slough's reputation at Chelsea was Ray Waite, who has since been responsible for equally magnificent displays by the Grounds of Reading University, and has now joined the Society as Superintendent of the Glasshouses at the RHS Garden at Wisley.

The sad decline in local authority exhibits in recent years is yet another example of the way in which Chelsea reflects social change. Under increasing political pressure to cut spending to the bone, it becomes more difficult to justify this use of ratepayers' money for a purpose that some would regard as frivolous and unnecessary, although in many circles the contribution made by parks departments to the urban environment is being seen as increasingly important.

The marquee offers to visitors not only the opportunity for horticultural enrichment in the general sense, but also the availability of specific scientific information and advice. The staff of Wisley Garden are in attendance throughout the Show at the Horticultural Information Bureau, where they give free advice on cultural difficulties, pests, diseases and other gardening problems to all visitors, whether members of the RHS or not.

Other exhibitors here may include the Agricultural Research Council, giving details of work carried out at five government research institutions throughout the country — work that ranges from the breeding of new raspberry and blackcurrant varieties to the identification of biological weapons, including bacteria and fungi, that are effective against common plant pests. There may even be an offering from the National Institute of Medical Herbalists describing the use of mosses, ferns, aromatic flowers, shrubs and tree leaves in modern herbal medicine.

Finally, in the North West corner of the marquee you come across the Garden Layout Section where landscape designers display samples of their work with plans and photographs of gardens, the experienced sealing their work against the ruinously damp atmosphere!

As well as individual designers and landscape companies, there is an exhibit by the Commonwealth War Graves Commission, to bring to the attention of visitors the extensive work of maintaining the thousands of graves of casualties from two world wars in many countries.

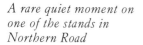

A rare quiet moment on one of the stands in Northern Road

From this quiet corner you may be tempted to venture once again on a circuit of the whole marquee, for there will always be something that you missed the first time around — a single flower or a whole stand that is so striking in its beauty it deserves to be seen again. But if you venture outside into Northern Road, it is possible to enjoy the complete contrast of a wealth of up-to-the-minute machinery, greenhouses and accessories that its exhibitors have to offer. Having seen with your own eyes the perfection that can be achieved by skilled and dedicated growers, now is your chance to review some of the equipment available to assist in your efforts to imitate their horticultural prowess!

Of the greenhouses, choose from a modest, basic six by eight foot house for something over £100 or a small but stylish circular house, or lavish rather more than £1,000 on a sturdy, spacious structure up to fifteen or twenty feet long with all mod cons — potential there for many happy hours of pottering.

There are conservatories, too, notably the traditional elegance of solid, white painted timber conservatories by Amdega, formerly the long-established firm of Richardsons of Darlington.

The traditional names in lawnmowers and machinery are still there too — Dennis, Qualcast, Wolseley Webb, Mountfield, Hayter and Allen — but these days many of the machines shown by the younger manufacturers are likely to

A typically crowded scene in Eastern Avenue

have been made in Japan, Australia or New Zealand, their engines in the United States or Italy. Nevertheless, it is fascinating to see their abilities demonstrated and explained enthusiastically, and a good opportunity to compare models.

Northern Road leads into Eastern Avenue via Main Way and the florists, and as you move along with the crowd, it may strike you that there is probably nowhere else on earth where, as well as gardens and flowers and plants for all seasons, you can see the whole world of gardening products, and almost everything associated with gardens, either on show or for sale.

Eastern Avenue at the Chelsea Show is like a cross between an Eastern Bazaar and Fifth Avenue, New York, offering the informality of a village market and the authority of Bond Street or Knightsbridge. There are books — both the latest offerings and secondhand and antiquarian delights hidden in dusty, faded jackets — on everything from Japanese gardens to organic vegetable cultivation. There are garden tools, some made from sparkling stainless steel; humble gloves, wellington boots and balls of string; hoses, ladders, sprinklers, trolleys, barrows, incinerators and compost bins. Then there are ornamental outdoor lamps and pond equipment; chemicals and fertilizers that offer, through modern scientific research, crop care and protection that is easy, effective and safe. Lovers of the flower garden can find accessories for floral art, pictures made from dried flowers and herbal pillows, cushions and scents. You can support the Royal Society for the Blind by buying a plant holder or trug, join the Sweet Pea Society or the National Trust and even book a long distance horticultural tour to an 'area of floral interest'.

At the bottom of Eastern Avenue, eagerly clutching those purchases they could not resist, visitors find themselves once again approaching the Chelsea Embankment. There may be time for a visit to the Floral Display Tent — if the queue is not too long — for another quick look around, for a much-needed rest in Ranelagh Gardens or a cup of tea before starting the long trek home. The flowers will soon be faded, but the memories of the sights, sounds and perfumes of the Chelsea Flower Show, its atmosphere and beauty will linger — until next year.

CHAPTER 7

THERE CAN hardly be better proof than Chelsea of the value in that old showbiz advice, 'Always leave your audience wanting more.' Every year, some visitors — and many would-be visitors — feel saddened or frustrated by the transient nature of this all-too-brief array of horticultural splendour. But if the proceedings were extended, exhibitors of plants, particularly of short-lived cut blooms, would face practical difficulties, and hardly any would welcome the inclusion of the Spring Bank Holiday weekend in the Show's open days.

However, some compensation for its transience can be found in the conscientious manner in which the exhibits are unfailingly recorded for posterity, by the written and spoken word, in photographs and on film. The interest of the Press and media seems to grow year by year, and with it their apparently insatiable thirst for information. The daunting responsibility for dispensing this information lies in the main with Miss Mildred Hobbs, the Society's Press Officer since 1964.

In a world where crisis and tragedy seem to be the constantly recurring themes of a journalist's work, it is understandable that coverage of the Chelsea Flower Show has become so popular. Its self-contained world is one of beauty, hope and optimism; its underlying theme the dependability of nature and the

Press day, before the crowds arrive, time and space for some serious photography

possibility of finding peace of mind in the innocent activity of gardening, and sharing that joy with fellow enthusiasts.

Mildred Hobbs prepares Press information for all the Society's shows, but finds that Chelsea is always in the back of her mind, whatever the time of year. Her work generally starts in November, when requests from the foreign Press begin to arrive, usually for general articles on the Show, with perhaps one or two tasters of the plans of the most forward-looking exhibitors.

Enquiries come from Australia, New Zealand, South Africa and the United States — but not only from English speaking countries, for keen interest in Chelsea is now shown by Germany, Italy, France, Belgium, Holland and Sweden among others. Nor do the requests for information come only from journalists. London's most famous hotels, for example, also want details to pass on to tourists who find themselves in town during Chelsea week.

A few weeks before the Show, Miss Hobbs circulates a major Press release, running to some ten pages or more, giving details of as many exhibits as possible, and based on information supplied by the exhibitors themselves. In some cases, obtaining advance information from exhibitors is like getting blood out of the proverbial stone. This is either because — with the endearing and typical lack of cut and thrust in the horticulturist's approach to business — they just 'didn't get around to it', or because they are reluctant to commit themselves in advance. It seems almost to be tempting providence to specify which plants will be shown, when some freak of nature could so easily strike.

Although Miss Hobbs always emphasises that the information given is about what exhibitors *hope* to show, there is some justification in this apprehension, for the weather and other unforeseen circumstances can drastically affect one's plans. Ron Sargent remembers occasions when exhibitors have had to drop out altogether at the last minute, through a transport strike in one instance and a nasty attack of bud drop in sweet pea plants (caused by cold or damp) in another.

The advance information is used in the preparation of Show previews by national and local newspapers, specialist gardening magazines and home interest publications, and many others. Often, at the Society's suggestion, they encourage readers to see the Show early or late in the day, when it is less crowded, and remind them that children under five are not admitted.

Having written so far only from advance information, journalists turn out in force on the Monday of Chelsea week to see how the reality compares, for as well as being the day of judgement and the Royal visit, this is Press Day. Members of the Press understand that many exhibitors are still working hard to complete their stands on Monday morning, but they can usually spare the time to give their inside story. It is a story that will be published anything up to three months later, but most national papers carry a report the following morning — often accompanied by the customary picture of the Queen, a policeman or a young child admiring a flower. The weekly gardening magazines, for both amateur and professional gardeners, will publish their reports at the end of Chelsea week, with one notable exception. *Garden News* has established a proud tradition of completing copy and photographs for its first Show reports on Saturday evening, rushing them to its Peterborough base for printing, and

Speakers in the garden
. . . all ready for a live
radio broadcast from the
Show

having the Show issue on sale in Eastern Avenue when the gates open on Tuesday morning. Their enterprise even extends to offering a free carnation with every copy.

Any advance Press coverage is obviously good for exhibitors, for visitors not only seek out the stands that have been mentioned, but often also remember details of the exhibit that they have gleaned from the article. Some exhibitors go further out of their way to attract publicity than others, usually by means of the presence of a well-known personality at a certain time, when a 'camera call' is invited. The celebrity may have an interest in gardening (Keith Castle, Anna Ford, Penelope Keith) or may be launching a flower named after them — usually a rose. In recent years, rose namesakes have been launched for Nana Mouskouri, Susan Hampshire, Cleo Laine, Esther Rantzen's baby Emily and many more. Perhaps it would be indiscreet to attempt to distinguish between those ladies to whom the grower has paid a genuine and generous tribute, and those who have paid the grower several thousand pounds for the privilege!

A rose launch that was not without its complications was one which involved BBC presenter, Sue Lawley. Sue was expecting a baby around Chelsea time, but promised John Mattock, who had named the rose in her honour, that if the baby had not arrived, she would definitely be there on Monday morning. On the Saturday evening, Mattock received a telephone call to say that the baby had been born, but with the help of the BBC publicity department, a mass of roses and one or two photographers were despatched to the hospital, and pictures of new mother, baby and rose together made an irresistible popular news story.

At lunch time on Press Day, exhibitors can continue their last minute work with fewer interruptions, as selected members of the Press — mainly magazine editors and national paper gardening correspondents — go off to the Press Lunch in the President's tent, along with members of the RHS Council and Committees who are to judge the exhibits later in the day.

A guest of honour is, by tradition, the Minister of Agriculture, and — also by tradition — both Lord Aberconway and the Minister are required to make a short speech. On the occasion of Fred Peart's second attendance at the lunch, as Minister, he said how delighted he was to be at Chelsea, but just one thing had bored him — Lord Aberconway's remarks in praise of the Show, which were exactly the same as in the previous year. Unabashed, the President rose to thank Mr Peart, saying, 'I have never been so complimented in my life, as to think that the Minister has remembered so clearly what I said a year ago. It is really very nice . . .' — to be greeted by a roar of applause.

Thus was the tradition established of Lord Aberconway's perennial claim that 'This year's Show is better than ever.' Although it is a phrase that has passed into Chelsea folklore, it nevertheless expresses a conviction that the President firmly holds. 'The analogy,' he says, 'is with improvements in the time for running the mile. Although that is measurable, and Chelsea is not, they come to

The Royal progress is attended by a bevy of photographers, television cameramen and even a sound recordist

the same thing. Chelsea is better through the improvement of plant strains, leading to better cultivars; through better methods of cultivation and transporting, and through better ways of staging, encouraged by competition.'

Although many people read newspaper and magazine reports on the Show, a much larger number sees the attractions of Chelsea through the eyes of the television camera. News cameras are greatly in evidence on the occasion of the Royal visit, and reports are shown by BBC, ITV, a number of local stations and even more overseas broadcasting companies. A tradition has also been established for BBC 2 to broadcast a forty-five minute programme on the Wednesday evening, taking a much closer look at the Show. For the last few years this has been produced by Michael Lumley, who received a good deal of public attention when he was responsible for BBC Television's live coverage of the wedding of the Prince and Princess of Wales.

As one of a group of producers responsible for outside broadcast events, Michael Lumley's experience is in the presentation of a wide range of events in an interesting way rather than specifically in horticulture. Although the commentary of the Chelsea programme does not talk down to knowledgeable gardeners, his aim, he says, is 'To make Chelsea as colourful and interesting as possible to the largest audience. I am conscious of the fact that this is the only horticultural type of programme that many viewers would conceive of watching.' The style of programme he has developed is neither straightforward news, nor a documentary, which would involve weeks of filming and editing, but a reportage that combines qualities of both and offers both immediacy and some insight into stories behind the exhibits.

Advance plans start as soon as information on the exhibits comes through some months before the Show. With two or three months to go fundamental decisions are made such as who will present the programme. Gardening personality and writer Peter Seabrook has filled this role for several years and the production team relies a good deal on his knowledge of horticulture and experience of the trade. He is joined by a second presenter who may be an experienced television journalist but new to Chelsea, such as Jan Leeming, or a horticulturist who is familiar with the Show, such as Ashley Stevenson of the Royal Parks. Both Michael Lumley and Peter Seabrook maintain close contact with Mildred Hobbs and Allan Sawyer, for information on what exhibitors plan to show.

During the weekend before the Show opens, the BBC team takes up position on a large triangle of grass by the rock garden bank. Its four electronic cameras divide into two pairs. Two cameras will record in one location, while the other two prepare for another location, so that there is a leapfrog effect. Each camera has a cable that is its umbilical cord, physically linking it with the central control vehicle, where the producer can see the master control picture and is in communication with cameramen and presenters. Exhibitors often wonder why the presence of so many large vehicles, miles of cable and numerous personnel is necessary. Michael Lumley explains that each camera is also connected by cable to a separate vehicle which records sound and pictures on video tape recording machines. A third vehicle is the generator to supply power for all the

A BBC camera team is stationed among the flowers . . .

OPPOSITE

. . . to record Peter Seabrook's expert view of the exhibits

equipment, and a fourth the tender which mainly carries cables but also takes technical equipment and incidentally provides shelter from heavy rain.

The production team already has a series of ideas for features in the programme, but at the Show final decisions are made as to the length each one warrants, whether interviews with exhibitors work in the time available and so on. Much as the information and advice from the RHS is needed and valued, these are decisions made with complete journalistic freedom but with one overriding restricting factor — the race against time.

The other restrictive factor is the purely physical one of the accessibility of cameras, and because of this coverage is limited mainly to marquee exhibits and the outside gardens. However, this may change in future with the anticipated introduction of electronic news-gathering cameras which need no cable.

Electronic recording on the stands inside the marquee takes place on Monday and very early on Tuesday morning, before the Show is open. When it is open, concealed cameras on stands or in entrances take sequences of visitors admiring exhibits in the marquee. Brief extracts from these will add life and atmosphere to the final programme. Recording pictures of the outside gardens now takes

place on Tuesday morning. Although it is more difficult for the cameras to move around, Michael Lumley feels that it is better to have a background of visitors looking at the gardens than of vehicles and people still working on their exhibits.

Although no major disaster has ever occurred, minor irritations are frequent. Aircraft noise is a problem, as anywhere in London, and on the ground there may be the hammering of posts or testing the public address system. Another difficulty is the sound of moving water. 'Water,' says Michael Lumley, 'has a sound that is all pervasive to the microphone. Some fountains, if they are not in shot, make the location sound more like a bathroom than a garden!'

As for weather, the programme makers can work in any conditions but the effect will be less than enhanced by water on the lens and the sound of falling rain in the background. Worse still is a combination of extremes. It would make a nonsense of continuity if Chelsea were to be seen one minute in brilliant sunshine and the next in pouring rain. One of the most drastic effects of bad weather is dismal light, particularly in the marquee, but if artificial light is used in one spot it throws the whole background out of balance. 'We try for the most faithful reproduction of colour,' says Michael Lumley, 'but in the end everything is a compromise because we are working against the clock.'

Time finally runs out around lunchtime on Tuesday, when everybody dashes back to Television Centre and the production team proceeds to assemble bits and pieces of video tape. The programme is usually assembled as a series of pictures and the commentary then added, consisting of a mixture of sound recorded at the Show and additional material recorded in the studio — sometimes within only five or ten minutes of the programme being transmitted to viewers who, it is hoped, will be quite unaware of the tension, excitement and last minute decisions that have gone into its preparation.

More recently, Michael Lumley and his team have also produced a programme that they call 'Growing for Gold'. This is broadcast on the Sunday before the Show and looks more deeply behind the scenes at the way in which exhibitors plan, prepare and make their stands. In addition, they are sometimes asked to record short features about Chelsea for another BBC programme — in one instance, unforgettable to Peter Seabrook, for the lunchtime programme from Birmingham, 'Pebble Mill at One'.

It was just before the time when the Royal family usually arrives on Monday afternoon, but because the exact moment cannot be predicted and every minute is precious to Michael Lumley's team, they were working quickly to record the Pebble Mill feature before rushing to be at the gate for the Queen's arrival. This involved Peter Seabrook walking along the Embankment avenue, by the rock gardens, and speaking an introduction. A microphone cable had already broken, causing some delay, and adding to the tension, so he was using a radio microphone tucked inside his jacket and the camera was positioned some distance away. To the casual observer, he appeared to be talking into mid-air, and a passing dustcart had already been hastened out of his way, having positioned itself between Peter and the camera. He had, moreover, removed the vital ticket authorising his presence during the Royal visit and was soon approached by a Special Constable, who told him smartly to leave. 'But,' replied an agitated Peter, 'I'm recording a piece for a television programme. Will you stand aside for a moment.'

'I don't care,' persisted the officer. 'Where's your badge?' 'Look, if I don't finish this recording in the next two minutes, the programme will never be done. Please step aside.'

'No I won't,' came the still persistent reply. 'I don't care what you're doing. I want to see your badge.' At this point the tension of the occasion proved too much for both men and an extremely heated exchange took place that eventually involved both the officer and his superior. Four million Pebble Mill viewers never did get a glimpse of Chelsea, 'But,' explains Michael Lumley with a wry grin, 'we certainly had an interesting piece of tape.'

The Wednesday evening programme has an obvious impact on viewers who visit the Show on the Thursday and Friday. They often go out of their way to find exhibits that have been featured, and enquire about interesting plants or items that have been explained. On more than one occasion, exhibitors have overheard the father of a family explaining a point to his wife and children as though he were imparting a gem of inside information to which only he is privy!

The BBC too receives a large number of letters, usually asking for more information about something that has been mentioned, but sometimes simply saying thank you for an enjoyable programme. Occasionally there is criticism, too, such as the half-dozen or so people who noticed that for the first time ever orchids had not been shown.

The widespread Press and media coverage of Chelsea emphasises its importance not only to the public but also to the horticultural trade for the Show is, quite simply, its largest shop window. Nurserymen are able to launch new plants in a blaze of publicity and smaller, specialist growers have been known to make their reputation at the Show, where they can stimulate quite a following for hitherto little-known or neglected plants. Adrian Slack and his carnivorous plants is one example; Beth Chatto and her rich texture of foliage plants for dry places is another. Manufacturers of garden sundries and equipment are more likely to launch new products to the trade in autumn so that home gardeners can buy and use them the following spring, but leisure goods such as barbecues and furniture sometimes receive a public launch at Chelsea, as do landscaping accessories such as sheds and summerhouses, paving and walling. Even if they are not showing brand-new products, manufacturers still value the opportunity for direct contact with their most knowledgeable and discerning customers. The comments, enquiries, suggestions and even criticism they receive can be extremely useful, as well as the more obvious boost to sales.

It is not only those who exhibit but the trade as a whole that benefits from Chelsea. Its bountiful array of perfect blooms with their nuances of perfume and colour, and of meticulously-tended gardens; its spirit and atmosphere are enough to soften the heart of even the most hardened reluctant gardener. The interest that it stimulates reverberates throughout the whole gardening world.

Just after that first ever exhibition held in the grounds of the Royal Hospital in 1912, Messrs James Carter & Co wrote a letter to the *Gardener's Chronicle* that could be considered quite prophetic, for as far as Chelsea exhibitors are concerned, the sentiments expressed still hold true today:

'But what of the exhibitors and the sacrifices they have made? Will a compensation accrue affording them satisfaction? We have no hesitation in saying that such will be the case. There is no finality in horticulture. This event which has brought together so many exhibitors from so many countries in presenting before the public the very best, the most beautiful and the most perfect forms in flower fruit and shrub will prove to be an education to the many thousands who passed the turnstiles and examined the exhibits. An educated appreciation of horticultural pursuits means a greater demand for the "best", and means in the long run "better trade". This is the return which we anticipate will come to exhibitors, and which, in our opinion, is the best return possible.'

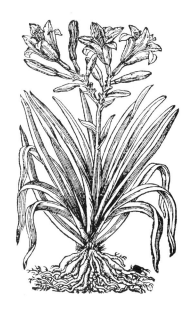

CHAPTER 8

 HELSEA SHOW week seems to pass by all too quickly. Exhausting though it is to be on duty on a stand, even for part of the time, it is also somehow exhilarating. There are always old friends to see and for gardeners it is the best place in the world to meet new friends who share and understand your interests. The Show grounds are like a self-contained village, with its own hierarchy and sense of community. The long opening hours leave everyone who works there with a feeling of isolation from everyday life that is not unpleasant.

Each night, after the crowds have gone, we put away the leaflets, tidy the garden, sweep the paths and paving and water the plants, savouring the cool quiet of the evening and the smell of damp grass and leaves. Marquee exhibitors check their blooms, replacing those that have faded with fresh supplies, usually on Wednesday night. As we drive home over Albert Bridge, bathed in the glow of the illuminations adorning its parapets, there is time to glance back for a glimpse of the heavy metal railings and gates, the peaked roof of the marquee with flags gently fluttering in the dusk, and to feel a sense of pride in belonging — in being a part of it all. Over the bridge and the moment is gone. Driving through the dull streets of Battersea and Balham, we return to wondering whether our feet and voices will hold out for another day.

All exhibitors are tempted to wonder at times whether the long months of preparation, the days of staging and the endless hours of answering enquiries are really worth it, but the feeling is only experienced in the lowest and weakest moments — the time when disaster strikes, when carefully-laid plans come to grief or when it is pouring with rain and bitterly cold. In our heart of hearts, we know we cannot stop coming because the special, unique experience of the Chelsea Show becomes compulsive. As one exhibitor says, 'Chelsea gets in your blood.' Others admit that even if their participation resulted in no profit to their business, they would still not be able to stay away.

The organisers, too, understand this. Ron Sargent, who saw so many Chelseas between 1934 and 1978, recalls: 'During my time at the Royal Horticultural Society I felt a little unhappy on just one or two occasions, but on the whole I enjoyed my work there. Although there were other shows throughout the year, there was always something to do with Chelsea on the go.'

Certainly the site has its limitations and ironically it is the extent of the Show's popularity that has caused it to come in for criticism, with suggestions from some quarters that the RHS should find for it a new, larger home — if necessary out of London. The Show's devotees have deep emotional reasons for wanting it to remain in the grounds of the Royal Hospital, but its organisers cannot afford to indulge in mere emotion; there are genuine practical and economic arguments for the Great Spring Show to remain on the site it has occupied since 1913. In July 1981 the President of the Royal Town Planning Institute and others wrote a letter to *The Times*, suggesting that the RHS should move the Chelsea Flower Show around the country from year to year. The President, Lord Aberconway replied thus:

'We stage the Chelsea Show in the most practicable place. No other site that we know of in this country (and we have considered many) has the convenience of location and ease of access combined with necessary facilities: internal roads, electricity, water, gas for cooking, sewerage, storm drains. Our skilled staff, experienced in the problems and routines of our present site, organize the show each year impeccably. But if we were to try to stage it, even for one year, in another place (let alone a different place each year) our staff would need to be greatly increased, problems would be formidable, mistakes and omissions would be inevitable and the cost would rise astronomically, making a nonsense of our hitherto successful efforts to keep the society, with its many activities besides Chelsea, economically viable.'

So, for the foreseeable future at least and we hope for many years yet, the South Grounds of the Royal Hospital, Chelsea play host to this proud and unique meeting of people and plants for the third week of every May.

On the last day of that week there is a distinct 'end of term' feeling. Friday is always very busy and the crowd is a mixture of really keen gardeners and those who have just come out of curiosity, to enjoy the spectacle and atmosphere. During the afternoon, while the exhibitors begin to relax and wind down it is among the visitors that the tensions starts to mount, for there is another reason for the presence of many — the search for a bargain. Here, at five o'clock on Friday afternoon is the sale to end all sales, as many exhibitors dispose of the plants that they have tended with such loving care. Although perhaps sad to see

Picking over the blooms

A deal is struck

118

them go, they can at least be assured that their protegees will be the object of great pride and appreciation in many a suburban garden.

Chelsea on Friday evening — better than a day at the sales

With a couple of hours to go, the prospective buyers start to plan their moves, sidling up to the stands and asking, 'Will you be selling your plants?' If the answer is yes and the plants and prices are right, they are likely to return at half-past-four and stand vigil over the prize they hope to claim for a full half hour. If the answer is no there is sometimes pleading and cajoling, perhaps turning eventually to indignation. The determined gardener is a force to be reckoned with. But often the plants are simply not ours to sell, or are too valuable to part with at bargain prices. All around the marquee it is much the same story. Some exhibitors sell nothing, others retain only their stock plants and special show specimens, and others again sell cut blooms or seasonal plants that have been forced into flower and would otherwise only be thrown away. But the visitors don't seem to worry. Whether genuine bargains or simply short-lived souvenirs, they earmark mentally the objects of their desire, hovering nonchalantly near the stands with an air of barely-contained excitement and anticipation.

Just after four o'clock, over the public address system with cool, refined aplomb comes the firm reminder that *no* plants are to be removed from the stands until the bell goes at five o'clock. Exhibitors are grateful for this timely reinforcement of their position, and their would-be customers just manage to maintain an air of forced dignity, knowing only too well that the moment the bell begins to ring all caution and reserve will be thrown to the wind and it will be every man, every woman for themselves in glorious, total abandon.

Under starters' orders and they're pressing forward now. The determination is really showing in their eyes, the notes rustling in their hands, the arms almost outstretched. Suddenly the loud ringing begins, everybody starts momentarily at the noise, then they're off!

119

Flowers are whipped from vases by the handful, plants are pulled from the stands, and heaved out of the ground. Money changes hands so quickly there is hardly time to see it and exhibitors run back and forth between the front and back of their stands with bundles of plants in boxes, newspapers, carrier bags. Once again comes a refined announcement, 'Ladies and gentlemen, the Show is now closed . . . .' but the message is ignored, drowned by the clamour of anxious voices. 'You promised those to me', 'I was here before them', 'I don't want a red one, I want a white one', 'The geraniums are cheaper over there' and, pathetically, 'I'm only a pensioner, dear.' (Invariably it works.)

Of course, it is one thing to buy — often on sheer impulse — and quite another to get your purchases home. The gargantuan task is undertaken by every possible means. The determined gardener is hardy and does not readily accept defeat. The booty is carried on the head or shoulder, in the arms, under the arm or on the back. In bags, boxes and on barrows — for those lucky enough to find them — it is dragged, heaved, shoved and even rolled. Not only plants — there are tables and chairs, ornaments, pots and even pieces of rock.

We well remember the sight of an elderly lady sitting on a chair in the middle of the grass verge of Main Avenue, surrounded by bags and parcels full of plants — more than she could possibly carry — and saying in a small, bewildered voice, 'I've got to get the train back to Liverpool tonight.' Some bring their car to the Bull Ring or try for a bus. As for the taxi drivers, they don't know whether to laugh or cry or just take the money and clean the cab later. The saying goes that you don't need to ask the way back to Sloane Square station on the last night of Chelsea — just follow the trail of delphinium petals.

The police on duty at the Bull Ring gate can barely suppress their laughter, even though they have seen it all before. They must prevent plant-laden cars from blocking the road by the entrance, but approach their task in a fairly tolerant and relaxed mood, for it is impossible not to be swept along by the hectic, carnival atmosphere.

The pushing, shoving, scurrying, the shouting and bargaining are soon over and as the crowds make their way home, we have a chance to stop and look around at the pitiful devastation that is left. Two hours ago, there was a stupendous array of charm and beauty. Now there is the turmoil of peat, mud, empty pots, half-pillaged stands and plant beds, and suddenly the exhaustion and the dejection bite. As Mr Bromage says, 'Chelsea is a magnificent Show because so many people love it so much. Love goes into every stand that is built.' When you pull that stand to pieces, it is like destroying a part of yourself.

But the sad business of clearing up must begin. Every exhibitor must obtain from the RHS a Certificate of Clearance to state officially that their exhibit has been cleared and the space tidied to the satisfaction of the Society, who must in turn account for themselves to the Royal Hospital. For the drivers of vans and lorries that will collect the sorry remains, the clearing process has started some hours previously, over the river in Battersea Park. Each one displays an official sticker on its windscreen — a different colour for each category of exhibitor — and each group is marshalled by the police into a relatively orderly queue to await the trek across the great divide. There is nothing to do but wait — to sit in

*Now how are we going
to get them home?*

*Determined gardeners
carry off their spoils*

'Do you think we've bought too much?'

the cab and read, snooze or drink tea from a flask; to stretch the legs and gaze across the River Thames and maybe chat with fellow drivers.

Eventually, at the given moment, just as London is pouring homeward for the Spring Bank Holiday weekend, a police escort emerges from Battersea Park, lights flashing, and behind it follows a convoy of large lorries and modest vans, shining new or dusty and choking. They all snake slowly over Chelsea Bridge, around to the Bull Ring and into the Show ground, where commences the slow progress around the one-way system. Lorries for the stands in Eastern Avenue enter first, followed by vehicles belonging to the Marquee exhibitors. Their stands do not take long to clear, as everybody pitches in with a will to heave, carry and barrow the plants in the opposite direction from that in which they came just seven or eight long days ago. Along the now multi-directional gangways are strewn squashed and broken flowers, leaves and pieces of twig, string and paper. Soon the wooden tables and trestles revert to boring normality, their hour of glory gone.

The rubbish containers that are delivered at intervals around the grounds soon become full to overflowing. They are supplied by the official site contractor, A & J Bull of Mitcham who before, during and after the Show are responsible for keeping the site clean and tidy. The job has been done by this family firm — now a large business concern — since the first Chelsea Show, as well as for the 1912 exhibition. In the early days, horse drawn carts would travel around the Show, clearing rubbish and sprinkling cinders on the avenues in wet weather, for the roads were still unmade. One of the firm's earliest motor lorries was on display in a corner of the grounds at a recent Chelsea Show.

124

Now, 'skip lorries' with automated lifting gear carry the rubbish containers, both on behalf of the RHS and for individual exhibitors. Those who show gardens or outdoor stands in the open either undertake to clear their own site, or contract A & J Bull to carry out this work.

On Friday evening, as more and more vehicles enter the grounds and movement around the roadways becomes almost impossible, it is the turn of the garden exhibitors' transport to enter last of all, in order to clear only plants and smaller, precious items that cannot be left. The actual dismantling and demolition of walls (including every vestige of their foundations), tearing up of paving and ponds and removal of buildings must wait until the weekend, and must be completed by Wednesday of the following week.

Dusk is falling as we eventually, wearily load plants on to the lorry. Numbly, we walk back and forth over filthy paving strewn with mud and peat, leaves and petals — paving that was this afternoon a neat, clean little patio. It may be nearly dark by the time we have finished and see the driver on his way, and then comes the walk to our own car, still at the front of the Royal Hospital. More than once, we have chosen the wrong gate to try and gain access to Royal Hospital Road. Laden with bags, parcels and plants, and on one occasion even a statue, we hardly know whether to laugh or cry as the great gate looms, firmly closed and padlocked. There is nothing for it but to walk right around to the other exit or stand and shout, risking the wrath of the officer on duty.

With a heavy heart, struggling to stay awake, we glance back from Albert Bridge for the last time. Tomorrow, the marquee will still be there and the commissionaires will be back in their caravan at the gate, but the grounds will

The Show is over

look like a battle ground when the armies have collected their dead. The gardens will be devastated and without a single bloom, their walls standing silent and dirty, their canvas screens torn and loosely flapping. The only sound will be the monotonous thud of pick on concrete or a sheet of polythene rustled along Main Avenue by a chilling wind.

It would all be too sad for words were it not for one thing — the hope, the promise, the certainty that when summer and winter have passed, when spring has reached the maturity of early May, then slowly, leaf by young green leaf, petal by soft petal, the Chelsea Flower Show will unfold to bloom all over again.

INDEX